Mars and *Venus* IN TOUCH

Enhancing the Passion with Great Communication

THE BEST OF *MARS AND VENUS*
COMPILED EXCLUSIVELY FOR HALLMARK

JOHN GRAY, Ph.D.

HarperCollins*Publishers*

Published under license from HarperCollins Publishers Inc.

FIRST EDITION

ISBN 0-06-095546-5

00 01 02 03 04 RRD 10 9 8 7 6 5 4 3 2 1

Contents

Foreword

I am delighted that with this Hallmark Books presentation of *Mars and Venus In Touch*, readers can once again, or for the very first time, learn how we as men and women can better communicate and understand one another.

The tremendous success of *Men Are from Mars, Women Are from Venus* and the *Mars and Venus* books that have followed, is living proof that, while we all experience the frustration of not being able to successfully communicate our thoughts and wishes to the opposite sex, most of us continue to hold the hope that we will find new and better ways to reach and understand each other.

In fact, the secret of creating lasting passion is to first understand our own unique needs, and then to understand the different needs of our partner. Quite often, when we fall in love, passion is automatic because we assume that we are going to get all of our needs met, despite the fact that we don't as of yet know the person we think we love. Passion dims when we discover that this person is not perfect and cannot possibly meet all of our needs.

In truth, real love doesn't demand perfection. Real love is accepting and understanding our partners, imperfections and all. This is only possible if we can first learn to identify our own needs, and ask for what we want in our relationship and in our life. Having done that, we discover that a greater awareness of our partner's needs gives us the power to re-ignite and sustain the passion of our relationship.

Through the development of new communication skills, you will not only get what you need for yourself in your relationship, but you will gain increased patience and wisdom to learn your loved one's needs as well. As a basic rule of thumb, men will automatically give to a woman what a man values most, while a woman will give the support that she would respond to. But what he wants is not always what she wants. For example, a man commonly prioritizes sex in the relationship, so he assumes that this is what is important to her. In reality, a woman may have many more prerequisites—such as affection, communication, or understanding—before her other desires.

As in my other *Mars and Venus* books, which deal with the various ages and stages of relationships, on these pages you will find practical solutions that will allow you to grow together in love. The conflict that you experience won't disappear, but will be explained and therefore contained. When there is tension in a relationship, it is very common for loving partners not to know what to do to make things better. *Mars and Venus In Touch* will provide you with a communications road map that will help you take the journey back to better understanding.

When we allow ourselves to forget our essential differences, we invite into our relationships a needless degree of confusion and frustration. When one partner realizes that the other partner has a need to share feelings or an urge to offer solutions, when one partner is driven to communicate but the other partner wants to retreat, it does not make the differences dissolve, but it melts much of the tension and frustration that those differences cause. These new insights into the differences between us raises our individual self-esteem and, at the same time, inspires mutual trust, personal responsibility, increased cooperation, and greater love.

All of the principles in this book have been tested and tried. As a result of questioning more than 25,000 participants in my relationship seminars, I have been able to define, in positive terms, how men and women are emotionally different. Over 90 percent of these participants have openly and enthusiastically recognized themselves in these descriptions. When you recognize those common themes both in yourself and in your soul mate you realize instantly that you are not alone. Unrealistic expectations are easily corrected, allowing you to create the love that you deserve.

There really is a reason why he does not want to ask for directions, and a reason why his telephone skills leave something to be desired. At the same time, she needs to know that her lover is someone she can share her feelings with, and that this someone will be to her more than just a fair weather friend. She has her well; and he has his cave.

But don't let those misunderstandings fool you. A man may not know how to reach his partner, and a woman might be just as confused about her man, but more times than not, the anger they feel is frustration—not a lack of love. You can use the love that you feel for each other as the foundation for building on the new skills you will find on these pages.

Opening the heart results in greater forgiveness and increased motivation to give and receive love and support. By opening yourself and your partner to a new level of understanding, you will go beyond the suggestions in this book and continue to develop ways in which you can relate lovingly to each other.

Through *Mars and Venus In Touch*, I hope that you will once again be inspired to reach for greater understanding in your search for true and lasting love.

If your relationship is just beginning or in its fiftieth year, the time is always right for us to learn how we can better please the one we love and, by so doing, make our love an example of how together we can make the world a better place.

1

Learning the New Language of Love

New Relationship Skills

Throughout this book, I will discuss in great detail the relationship skills necessary to support our partners' new emotional needs while getting exactly what we need to be happy and enjoy lasting intimacy and passion. Even if some of the ideas laid out here seem familiar or old-fashioned, they are being presented in dramatically fresh and different ways.

For example, instead of simply advocating that a woman be pleasing to her man, I suggest that she please him by letting him please her. Instead of passively waiting on him, she learns ways in which to get the support she needs.

In a sense, she is still required to help him, but with a new twist: She learns how to help him help her, how to support him in supporting her more, and how to accommodate him so that he will in turn accommodate her needs and wishes.

I suggest that men continue to be providers but with a new twist. By actually "doing less," a man can learn to provide the emotional support a woman needs. For example, instead of trying to provide solutions to a woman's problems, I suggest that he "do less" and learn to listen with empathy. While "listening with increasing empathy," it actually builds upon his ancient warrior skill of silently waiting and watching.

With the correct understanding, men can become adept in this new skill by using abilities that have taken centuries to develop. Using his warrior skills, he will learn to protect himself constructively when a woman speaks. The new twist is that he learns to defend himself *without* attacking his partner.

Relationships become increasingly difficult when we expect too much of ourselves or our partners. In education theory, to learn something new, you must hear it (and/or apply it) two hundred times. If you are a genius, maybe a hundred and fifty times will do. Mastering new relationship skills is not immediate.

Occasionally forgetting what you have learned is perfectly normal; old patterns and reactions do come back to haunt us. Now, you will understand your part of the problem instead of hopelessly blaming your partner or solely yourself. Changing for the better is sometimes hard work, but at each progressive step it will also become easier, more rewarding, and more fun. And, once learned, these skills will enrich all aspects of your life and your relationships.

Anticipating Setbacks

The most important relationship skill of all is anticipating temporary setbacks and acknowledging the necessity of re-learning a lesson until it becomes second nature. This understanding gives us the hope to be patient and the forgiveness to be loving.

Although learning all the new skills may seem overwhelming at times, the process is also very exciting. As you begin to practice new relationship skills, the immediate and tangible results will give you continued cause for hope, encouragement, and support. With your very first step on this journey, your relationships can dramatically and immediately improve, and gradually, with more practice, keep on getting better.

Through learning these essential skills you can achieve lasting passion, intimacy, and happiness. Passion does not have to dissipate, the happiness shared during the courting process does not have to fade, and intimacy can deepen into a source of increasing fulfillment. In the next section, we will explore what women need most, and men really want, if we are to experience lasting intimacy.

What Women Need Most and Men Really Want

The women who attend my relationship seminars are always amazed by the fact that half the audience is composed of men. They find it hard to believe, but men really are seeking ways to make women happy and are just as interested as women in improved relationships. The problem is that their traditional ways of doing so aren't getting through to the women.

If problems arise at home, the traditional male approach to solving them is to become more successful at work. If a relationship is troubled, a traditional man doesn't take a seminar or purchase a book on relationships; he takes a course or buys a book on business or success. Why? Because from time immemorial, a man could always make his partner happier by being a better provider.

In hunter/gatherer days, this arrangement worked out fine. It worked well enough even for our fathers. For us, however, it doesn't work at all. Today's wives do not leave husbands because they're not being provided for. They leave because they are emotionally and romantically unfulfilled. When a man does not understand a woman's new needs, it is inevitable that she will be unfulfilled. This increased dissatisfaction is also what turns men off. Husbands do not leave wives because they no longer love them, they leave because they can't make them happy. Generally speaking, a man gives up on a relationship when he feels powerless to succeed in fulfilling his partner.

By understanding how circumstances have changed for both

sexes, we can gain the insight and compassion necessary to master new approaches to mutually supportive relationships.

Why Modern Women Are Unhappy

Modern women are overworked, overstressed, and commonly feel unsupported and overwhelmed with good reason: At no other time in history has so much been expected of them. At least five days a week, they put on a uniform and march into an eight- to twelve-hour battle. When they come home, they feel the need to clean house, make dinner, do laundry, love and nurture the kids, and also be pleasing and happy as well as romantically receptive to their mates. It's just too much to ask of themselves, and it's making them feel split inside.

At work, women are required to behave according to the traditional masculine rules of conduct. At home, they have to switch to being warm, giving, and feminine. It's no wonder women complain that they need a wife to greet them with love and tenderness at the end of the day.

Even a contemporary stay-home mother has a more difficult job than her own mother did because, with most other mothers at work and her kids' playmates at day care, she lacks the traditional company and support of other women.

In the past, a woman was proud to say that she was a full-time wife and mother. Now she may even feel embarrassed when asked, "What do *you* do?" Isolated from the support of other women, she must go it alone, as the value of her commitment is largely unacknowledged by the world.

Still, while women now need more support than at any other time in history, men also miss the ego boost they traditionally received from their mates.

Why Men Are Dissatisfied

Modern men feel underpaid, defeated, and unappreciated. Like women, they are experiencing the toll that a two-career marriage takes.

Years ago, when a man returned to a stay-home wife she could easily show him how much she appreciated his efforts and sacrifices. Happy to care for him because she wasn't stressed out, she asked relatively little in return. Now, abruptly, the home as a male comfort base is under siege.

Many men work just as hard as their forefathers, perhaps even harder, but still can't manage to be their family's sole support. Deprived of the strong sense of self that being a sole provider would bring him, on a deep emotional (and sometimes unconscious) level he easily feels defeated when his partner seems unhappy or unfulfilled.

A Man's Primary Goal

When a man loves a woman, his primary goal is to make her happy. Through history, men have endured the competitive and hostile world of work because, at the end of the day, their struggles and efforts were justified by a woman's appreciation. In a very real sense, his mate's fulfillment was the reward that made a man's labor worthwhile.

Today, because women are overworked, they often and understandably feel unfulfilled. Now, at a long day's end, *both* she and her mate are looking for love and appreciation. "I work as hard as he does," she tells herself. "Why is it my responsibility to appreciate him?" Exhaustion now prevents her from giving her man the emotional support he knows he has earned.

To him, her unhappiness signals that he is a failure. "Why should I bother to do more?" he asks himself. "I'm unappreciated for what I do already." The harmful effects of this relatively new pattern are greatly underestimated by both women and men.

What Makes Women Happy

Years ago, when most women were full-time homemakers, a woman enjoyed the support of other women throughout the day. She could break up her tasks and relax by talking while giving and receiving in the spirit of cooperation, not competition. She had the luxury of unstructured time to create beauty in her home, garden, and community. She cared for others and they cared for her.

This daily routine was conducive to nurturing her feminine spirit and the love in her heart. Her caring relationships gave meaning to her existence and supported her through life's inevitable crises.

Women were not expected to shoulder the double burden of nurturing relationships and providing for the family. Men were happy to provide, and able to be sole providers, leaving their partners free to perform their tasks while creating and sustaining loving relationships. In the competitive and hard-driving male-dominated workforce of today, this emphasis on relationships is greatly missing, and for the first time in history women are being forced to do without the support of being in a nurturing and feminine environment.

Imitation Men

One woman in my seminar expressed her feelings in this way: "I feel like an imitation man. Women in the workforce have no female role models for success. I don't know how a woman can be expected to be strong and assertive and feminine at the same time. I'm losing touch with who I really am."

When women spend their days behaving in traditionally masculine roles, it is tremendously difficult to remain feminine. Working on a very structured timetable, making decisions based primarily on the bottom line and not people's feelings, giving orders when there is no time to share the decision-making, calculating strategic moves to protect herself from attack, creating alliances based solely on profit margins and not on friendship, investing time and energy for personal gain rather than others' benefit, all contribute to the impoverishment of the feminine soul.

Women at Work and at Home

Women are affected much more adversely than men by career stress, for the pressures of work outside the home have doubled their load. On the job, they give as much as men do, but when they get home, instinct takes over and they continue giving.

It is hard for a woman to come home, forget the problems of the day, and relax when her programming says, "Cook more, clean more, love more, share more, nurture more, give more, do more." Think of it. Tasks that used to fill a woman's whole day must now be done in a few hours. Along with providing, there is just not enough time, support, or energy to fulfill her biological yearnings for a beautiful, peaceful home and a loving, harmonious, and healthy family. She feels overwhelmed by too much to do.

Whether these instincts come from biology or from watching and identifying with her mother while growing up, they can be very strong. Many times these pressures increase when a woman begins planning for children or has children. While these feelings and pressures are self-induced, they are based on modern physical realities our mothers didn't have to deal with in their efforts to create a home and family. It is not only essential for women to learn new ways of coping, but for men to learn new ways to support their partners.

Men at Work and at Home

Through history, men could tolerate the stresses of the outside world because they would return home to a nurturing and loving woman. All day the male was goal-oriented, but come evening, he either relaxed, played, or was waited on with love. What he didn't have to do was continue working to win his partner's favor.

When a modern woman shares her feelings of having to do too much, a man generally hears it as blame for not doing enough or as an order to do more. Neither message is agreeable to his nature, which is telling him, "OK, you're home. Relax and reap the rewards of your labor."

Giving Requires Receiving

Men are wired to give their all to work, then come home and receive. To a great extent women are built to give and receive at the same time. They love to give but need to be fueled simultaneously: When they give without receiving, they tend to give more and eventually feel overwhelmed, empty, and resentful.

It follows that a woman who spends her day in a competitive, masculine workplace does not get the emotional support she would if she were in a more feminine, nurturing environment. She gives and gives at her job but doesn't receive validation and support. She comes home burned out, but instead of relaxing, she continues to give.

This is an important difference between men and women. When a man is tired, he will generally have a strong tendency to forget his problems and rest and relax. If he is not getting the support he needs, then he will tend to stop giving more. If he gives at work without getting back, then particularly when he gets home he feels ready to relax and receive for a while, or at least take some time for himself.

On the other hand, when a woman feels unsupported, she feels responsible for doing more and begins to think of or worry about all the problems she doesn't have the energy to solve. The more overwhelmed she feels, the more difficult it is for her to relax and put off the chores that just can't be done, and really don't have to be done right away.

When she feels overwhelmed, it is difficult for her to determine what really needs to be done and what can wait. In some cases, the expectations her mother had about how a home should be kept instinctively come into play. The more overwhelmed or unsupported she feels, the more these instincts come up. In a subconscious way she may be trying to live up to the standards of housekeeping and entertaining that were appropriate back when every wife was a homemaker and had the time and energy to do it all.

Particularly when a working woman cannot afford outside help for chores at home, she may begin to feel that she is just not doing enough. Instinctively she feels that she has to do more, yet realistically she can't do it all. It is as though she is gripped by out-of-date social programming that expects her to do it all at home.

In some cases, just as a woman feels responsible for doing it all at home, a man is socially programmed to feel that it is all her responsibility. Just as it is difficult for her to relax and do less, it is equally difficult for him to find the energy to help out.

Why Women Burn Out

Today, while men are away working, women are also away working; modern women don't have the time, energy, or opportunity to support each other as their mothers did. A modern woman will give and give, but because she is not feeling supported, she commonly returns home feeling burned out.

In addition, when a woman is dependent not on a man but

on her work to survive, her tendency to give freely is also restricted. If a women gives to make money, her support is not "freely offered." This manner of conditional giving further disconnects her from her femininity.

Working women are required to be overly masculine. They are no longer supported in expressing their femaleness through mothering, working together in cooperative and nurturing relationships, gathering (shopping), and homemaking. This tipping of the balance toward their masculine aspect is rapidly creating female burnout and dissatisfaction throughout the modern world.

The women of ancient days didn't burn out because their work environment nurtured their female nature. Women today burn out because they are not being sufficiently nurtured in their jobs.

Learning from the Wisdom of the Past

Traditionally, women felt proud of their biological roles, since mothering was highly honored, respected, and even considered sacred. In some cultures a woman was seen as being closer to God than a man, for she alone had been given the power to create life. Women were honored as the mothers, and men gladly became warriors, willing to risk their lives to provide for and protect the mothers of their children.

Going back just to my mother's generation, it is easy to find women who felt very good about themselves as mothers. I remember once as an adult asking my mother if she had liked being a mother. Her immediate response was, "Well, John, I still am a mother, and I still love it. I feel so fortunate to have seven beautiful children."

I was surprised that she so strongly and proudly identified herself as a mother even after her children were grown. I felt fortunate that she hadn't had to go to work and had truly enjoyed being a full-time mom with a husband to support her.

Most mothers today do not often have the luxury of full-time parenting. Having kids *and* having a job mandate a very difficult list of duties requiring new skills that your mother definitely could not have taught you. Without these strategies, the juggling of motherhood and career amounts to a tortuous trek through uncharted territory. Contemporary women considering motherhood are understandably hesitant.

While I am in no way suggesting that we turn back the clock and encourage women back into the kitchen, it is important that we understand what we have given up. As we stride forward on our quest for a new and better world for both women and men, we need to keep in mind the wisdom of the past and use it wherever applicable. Contained in that ancient wisdom are certain elements that are essential for female and male contentment. We should never lose touch with the ancient truths that have always enhanced female and male fulfillment.

Through understanding them, we can more effectively map out fresh approaches to relating that fulfill our instincts while allowing us to move ahead to new goals and dreams.

A Woman's Work Is Never Done

I remember a very telling conversation on the subject of contemporary motherhood. While I was signing books in a bookstore, three women and my wife were sharing stories about how difficult it is to be a mother today. When one woman disclosed that she was the mother of seven, another immediately gasped in admiration and sympathy.

"I only have two children," she said, "and I thought I had it bad. How do you do it?"

A third mother added, "I have only one child and that wears me out."

"I have three children," said my wife, "and I thought that was a lot. I can't imagine how you handle seven."

"Whether you have one, two, three, or seven kids, you give them everything you have," the mother of seven replied. "You only have so much to give, and every mother, no matter how many children she has, gives it all."

Suddenly the other three mothers realized that they were in effect doing the same job. They were each giving everything they had to give to mothering. They were following the ancient wisdom.

This insight completely changed my relationship with my wife. Before, when she complained about doing so much, I assumed she would never be happy until she learned to do less. Now I realized her doing too much was not the problem because she would always do all she could. Instead, I began to focus on finding ways to nurture her female side as she gave and gave. Not only was she happier, but because she felt so much more supported, she could indeed relax and do less.

Overgiving Is Not Dysfunctional

Giving too much becomes a problem only when a woman is not adept in getting back the nurturing support she needs to continue giving. Many popular books label women who give too much as "codependent" or dysfunctional when in many cases they are not. They are just following their healthy feminine instincts to give freely of themselves.

The more focused, responsible, competitive, and aggressive she is required to be at work, the more difficult it is for her to reconnect with the softness of her femininity when she gets home. It is then more difficult for her clearly to feel her needs. A woman will return home and continue thinking about the needs of others.

When a modern woman gets home she generally doesn't have the energy her mother had for domestic work. Instead of looking forward to and enjoying some nice "downtime," a woman, to various degrees, is driven to do more and can't relax. Although she instinctively feels she has to do more, she doesn't have the energy. This combination of feelings makes her feel suddenly exhausted and dissatisfied with her life.

The Nurture Cure

If an exhausted woman is given a big dose of nurturing, I assure you that she will get a second wind and not only more effectively cope with her need to act but actually enjoy it. When a woman feels exhausted, it is because she is not nurturing her female side.

This does not mean that women today don't need more help around the house. It is important that a man understand that modern women do require more support in the home. It is, however, also equally important that a woman understand that in some cases her expectations of what needs to be done in the home are unrealistic, given that they may be based on standards set by a generation of women who had more time for housework. While it is not fair to place those expectations on her male partner, it is also not fair for a man to ignore her legitimate need for more emotional support.

While the resolution of this problem will be different in every situation, the ability to resolve this potential conflict is based on mutual understanding, patience, and compassion.

What a Man Can Do

By allotting an extra twenty minutes three or four days a week, a man can do wonders to nurture a woman's female side. Not only will she be happier, but he will begin to get the appreciation and acceptance he needs when he gets home. No matter how overworked or exhausted she feels, he can, with a small amount of concentrated attention, focus his love and caring in ways that make a big difference.

Unless he comprehends the importance of nurturing a woman's female side, he may mistakenly leave her alone or try to persuade her to do less. Neither approach works, and may actually alienate her.

Simply trying to understand what her feelings are and what she goes through with some empathy or sympathy can have a tremendous nurturing effect on a woman's female side.

An overworked woman, with neither the time nor the opportunity to nurture her female side, may not even be aware of what she's missing; consequently, she may not know how to recapture her femininity. To do so, she needs a healthy dose of "relationship." Anything a man can do to nurture her female side will assist her in releasing her cares.

Through addressing this female side of her being, a man can respond compassionately and skillfully to a woman feeling exhausted and overwhelmed. Through clearly delineating her male and female aspects, he can effectively work at steering her toward "feeling like herself again."

A Perfect Fit

A woman can most successfully cope with the stress of experiencing non-nurturing relationships in the goal-oriented work world by coming home and experiencing a loving, caring, and cooperative relationship. The most important element of a nurturing relationship that she is generally missing at work is non-goal-oriented conversation. Through "talking" in a non-goal-oriented way, without having to get to the bottom line, without having to solve the problem, a woman is gradually released from the domination of her masculine side.

Talking in a nonlinear, unedited, emotional way is especially beneficial when her listener understands that by articulating her problems, she can put them aside.

That a woman can forget the problems of her day by remembering them is a concept foreign to most men, who generally banish the problems of the day by not talking about them. To bring them up in conversation, a man would have to address himself to solving them.

While it is important to men to *not* talk, it is equally important to women *to* talk. This apparent incompatibility is actually, we will find, a perfect fit.

When a woman needs to talk, it is not really necessary for a man to talk. In fact, if he talks too much, it can actually prevent her from opening up. When he thinks too much about what he is going to say, his mental focus shifts away from her.

Any man will listen when he is approached in the right way. Telling a man, "You never listen to me," or "We never talk, we should talk more!" is definitely taking the wrong tack. Such comments only make a man feel blamed, attacked, and defensive.

How to Get a Man to Listen

An approach my wife uses is simply to ask me to listen. She'll say, "Oh, I'm so glad you're home. I've had such a day. Would this be a good time to talk about it? (pause) You don't have to say anything. (little pause) I'm sure I'll feel better if I can just talk about it."

By inviting me to listen in this way, she gives me what I really want—a chance to make her happy—and she gets what she needs most—the opportunity to talk, share, and nurture her female side.

When women support their male partners in supporting them, everybody wins. With practice, sympathetic listening can eventually become easy for a man. Paradoxically, what women need most from men can be given with a minimum of effort.

Although listening in this special way is a new requirement for men in relationships, it is a talent we have spent thousands of years preparing for. Since the ancient hunter's major task was to watch and listen silently, men are good at it. Once he acquires the knack of applying this traditional talent to listening to his mate, a man can give a woman the special, focused attention she finds so wonderfully fulfilling.

The Art of Listening

The art of listening to a woman does not entail solving problems or offering advice. Conversely, a male listener's goal should be helping his partner regain her feminine/masculine balance.

This new job description clarifies his goal and thus guides him to watch and listen while giving her the sympathy she craves, not the solutions.

To develop skill in listening, a man needs to recognize that when a woman is upset and seems to be demanding solutions to her problems, it is only because she is still operating primarily from her male side. By not responding with solutions he assists her in finding her female side; she will then eventually feel better. Men are easily tricked into thinking that if they can give solutions women will then feel better.

Remembering this is particularly helpful when a man feels a woman is upset with him. To explain why she shouldn't be so upset with him only makes matters worse. Although he may have disappointed her in some ways, he must remember that her real complaint is that she is not being heard or nurtured as a woman. Then she will be capable of, and eager to bestow on him, the appreciation and acknowledgment that he has earned.

What Men Really Want

These days, when a man gets home, his wife not only is over-whelmed but is generally needy. She may have love in her heart, but he doesn't see it.

Deep in his soul, a man expects his woman to acknowledge and appreciate his efforts and in some measure be fulfilled by them. When she does not seem happy to see him, something very significant begins to happen. His tender but passionate desire to please her, protect her, and provide for her is dampened and is eventually snuffed out.

Men don't generally pinpoint what is happening inside themselves because they are more concerned with trying to make women happy. Yet the more a woman acts and reacts from feelings of unhappiness, something inside a man switches off. When his hard work seems to count for nothing, his life and relationship lose all magic and meaning for him.

Remember, what a man really wants is to make his partner happy; if he loves a woman, his primary goal is her fulfillment. Her happiness signals to him that he is loved. Her warm responses are like a mirror reflecting back to him a shining image.

Understanding Our Differences

This understanding of what men really want does not imply that a woman doesn't care about her partner's happiness as well. Certainly, when a woman loves a man, she wants him to also be happy, but note this crucial difference between men and women: A man can be stressed out from a day at work, but if his partner is happy with him, he feels fulfilled. When he senses her appreciation for his labor, his stress level dissipates; her happiness is like a shower that washes away the stressful grime of his day.

However, when an exhausted woman returns home to a

happy man, he doesn't make her day. It's great that he appreciates her hard work to help support the family, but it doesn't in the least diminish her unease. As we have discussed, she needs to communicate and feel some nurturing support before she can begin to appreciate him.

By understanding and honoring that men thrive on appreciation and women on communication, we gain the knowledge and the power to create mutually fulfilling relationships.

Even if you read only this chapter and apply these insights, your relationships will change forever for the better. To utilize this new understanding most effectively, we will explore a new job description for both partners in a relationship in the next chapter. Just as we must update our skills in business, so also do we need job retraining in our relationships.

2

Our Differing Emotional Needs

Men and women generally are unaware that they have different emotional needs. As a result they do not instinctively know how to support each other. Men typically give to relationships what men want, while women give what women want. Each mistakenly assumes that the other has the same needs and desires. As a result they both end up dissatisfied and resentful.

Both men and women feel they give and give but do not get back. They feel their love is unacknowledged and unappreciated. The truth is they are both giving love but not in the desired manner.

For example, a woman thinks she is being loving when she asks a lot of caring questions or expresses concern. As we have discussed before, this can be very annoying to a man. He may start to feel controlled and want space. She is confused, because if she were offered this kind of support she would be appreciative. Her efforts to be loving are at best ignored and at worst annoying.

Similarly, men think they are being loving, but the way they express their love may make a woman feel invalidated and unsupported. For example, when a woman gets upset, he thinks he is loving and supporting her by making comments that minimize the importance of her problems. He may say, "Don't worry, it's not such a big deal." Or he may completely ignore her, assuming he is giving her a lot of "space" to cool off and go into her cave. What he thinks is support makes her feel minimized, unloved, and ignored.

As we have already discussed, when a woman is upset she needs to be heard and understood. Without this insight into different male and female needs, a man doesn't understand why his attempts to help fail.

The Twelve Kinds of Love

Most of our complex emotional needs can be summarized as the need for love. Men and women each have six unique love needs that are all equally important. Men primarily need trust, acceptance, appreciation, admiration, approval, and encouragement. Women primarily need caring, understanding, respect, devotion, validation, and reassurance. The enormous task of figuring out what our partner needs is simplified greatly through understanding these twelve different kinds of love.

By reviewing this list you can easily see why your partner may not feel loved. And most important, this list can give you a direction to improve your relationships with the opposite sex when you don't know what else to do.

The Primary Love Needs of Women and Men

Here are the different kinds of love listed side by side:

Women need to receive	Men need to receive
1. Caring	1. Trust
2. Understanding	2. Acceptance
3. Respect	3. Appreciation
4. Devotion	4. Admiration
5. Validation	5. Approval
6. Reassurance	6. Encouragement

Understanding Your Primary Needs

Certainly every man and woman ultimately needs all twelve kinds of love. To acknowledge the six kinds of love primarily needed by women does not imply that men do not need these kinds of love. Men also need caring, understanding, respect, devotion, validation, and reassurance. What is meant by "primary need" is that fulfilling a primary need is required before one is able fully to receive and appreciate the other kinds of love.

A man becomes fully receptive to and appreciative of the six kinds of love primarily needed by women (caring, understanding, respect, devotion, validation, and reassurance) when his own primary needs are first fulfilled. Likewise a woman needs trust, acceptance, appreciation, admiration, approval, and encouragement. But before she can truly value and appreciate these kinds of love, her primary needs first must be fulfilled.

Understanding the primary kinds of love that your partner needs is a powerful secret for improving relationships on Earth. Remembering that men are from Mars will help you remember and accept that men have different primary love needs.

It's easy for a woman to give what she needs and forget that her favorite Martian may need something else. Likewise men tend to focus on their needs, losing track of the fact that the kind of love they need is not always appropriate for or supportive of their favorite Venusian.

The most powerful and practical aspect of this new understanding of love is that these different kinds of love are reciprocal. For example, when a Martian expresses his caring and understanding, a Venusian automatically begins to reciprocate and return to him the trust and acceptance that he primarily needs. The same thing happens when a Venusian expresses her trust—a Martian automatically will begin to reciprocate with the caring she needs.

In the following six sections we will define the twelve kinds of love in practical terms and reveal their reciprocal nature.

1. She Needs Caring and He Needs Trust

When a man shows interest in a woman's feelings and heartfelt concern for her well-being, she feels loved and cared for. When he makes her feel special in this caring way, he succeeds in fulfilling her first primary need. Naturally she begins to trust him more. When she trusts, she becomes more open and receptive.

When a woman's attitude is open and receptive toward a man he feels trusted. To trust a man is to believe that he is doing his best and that he wants the best for his partner. When a woman's reactions reveal a positive belief in her man's abilities and intentions, his first primary love need is fulfilled. Automatically he is more caring and attentive to her feelings and needs.

2. She Needs Understanding and He Needs Acceptance

When a man listens without judgment but with empathy and relatedness to a woman express her feelings, she feels heard and understood. An understanding attitude doesn't presume to already know a person's thoughts or feelings; instead, it gathers meaning from what is heard, and moves toward validating what is being communicated. The more a woman's need to be heard and understood is fulfilled, the easier it is for her to give her man the acceptance he needs.

When a woman lovingly receives a man without trying to change him, he feels accepted. An accepting attitude does not reject but affirms that he is being favorably received. It does not mean the woman believes he is perfect but indicates that she is not trying to improve him, that she trusts him to make his own improvements. When a man feels accepted it is much easier for him to listen and give her the understanding she needs and deserves.

3. She Needs Respect and He Needs Appreciation

When a man responds to a woman in a way that acknowledges and prioritizes her rights, wishes, and needs, she feels respected. When his behavior takes into consideration her thoughts and feelings, she is sure to feel respected. Concrete and physical expressions of respect, like flowers and remembering anniversaries, are essential to fulfill a woman's third primary love need. When she feels respected it is much easier for her to give her man the appreciation that he deserves.

When a woman acknowledges having received personal benefit and value from a man's efforts and behavior, he feels appreciated. Appreciation is the natural reaction to being supported. When a man is appreciated he knows his effort is not wasted and is thus encouraged to give more. When a man is appreciated he is automatically empowered and motivated to respect his partner more.

4. She Needs Devotion and He Needs Admiration

When a man gives priority to a woman's needs and proudly commits himself to supporting and fulfilling her, her fourth primary love need is fulfilled. A woman thrives when she feels adored and special. A man fulfills her need to be loved in this way when he makes her feelings and needs more important than his other interests—like work, study, and recreation. When a woman feels that she is number one in his life then, quite easily, she admires him.

Just as a woman needs to feel a man's devotion, a man has a primary need to feel a woman's admiration. To admire a man is to regard him with wonder, delight, and pleased approval. A man feels admired when she is happily amazed by his unique characteristics or talents, which may include humor, strength, persistence, integrity, honesty, romance, kindness, love, understanding, and other so-called old-fashioned virtues. When a man feels admired, he feels secure enough to devote himself to his woman and adore her.

5. She Needs Validation and He Needs Approval

When a man does not object to or argue with a woman's feelings and wants but instead accepts and confirms their validity, a woman truly feels loved because her fifth primary need is fulfilled. A man's validating attitude confirms a woman's right to feel the way she does. (It is important to remember one can validate her point of view while having a different point of view.) When a man learns how to let a woman know that he has this validating attitude, he is assured of getting the approval that he primarily needs.

Deep inside, every man wants to be his woman's hero or knight in shining armor. The signal that he has passed her tests is her approval. A woman's approving attitude acknowledges the goodness in a man and expresses overall satisfaction with him. (Remember, giving approval to a man doesn't always mean agreeing with him.) An approving attitude recognizes or looks for the good reasons behind what he does. When he receives the approval he needs, it becomes easier for him to validate her feelings.

6. She Needs Reassurance and He Needs Encouragement

When a man repeatedly shows that he cares, understands, respects, validates, and is devoted to his partner, her primary need to be reassured is fulfilled. A reassuring attitude tells a woman that she is continually loved.

A man commonly makes the mistake of thinking that once he has met all of a woman's primary love needs, and she feels happy and secure, that she should know from then on that she is loved. This is not the case. To fulfill her sixth primary love need he must remember to reassure her again and again.

Similarly, a man primarily needs to be encouraged by a woman. A woman's encouraging attitude gives hope and courage to a man by expressing confidence in his abilities and character. When a woman's attitude expresses trust, acceptance, appreciation, admiration, and approval it encourages a man to be all that he can be. Feeling encouraged motivates him to give her the loving reassurance that she needs.

The best comes out in a man when his six primary love needs are fulfilled. But when a woman doesn't know what he primarily needs and gives a caring love rather than a trusting love, she may unknowingly sabotage their relationship.

How You May Be Unknowingly
Turning Off Your Partner

Without an awareness of what is important for the opposite sex, men and women don't realize how much they may be hurting their partners. We can see that both men and women unknowingly communicate in ways that are not only counterproductive but may even be a turnoff.

Men and women get their feelings hurt most easily when they do not get the kind of primary love they need. Women generally don't realize the ways they communicate that are unsupportive and hurtful to the male ego. A woman may try to be sensitive to a man's feelings, but because his primary love needs are different from hers, she doesn't instinctively anticipate his needs.

Through understanding a man's primary love needs, a woman can be more aware and sensitive to the sources of his discontent. The following is a list of common communication mistakes women make in relation to a man's primary love needs.

<u>Mistakes women commonly make</u>	<u>Why he doesn't feel loved</u>
1. She tries to improve his behavior or help him by offering unsolicited advice.	1. He feels unloved because she doesn't *trust* him anymore.
2. She tries to change or control his behavior by sharing her upset or negative feelings. (It is OK to share feelings but not when they attempt to manipulate or punish.)	2. He feels unloved because she doesn't *accept* him as he is.
3. She doesn't acknowledge what he does for her but complains about what he has not done.	3. He feels taken for granted and unloved because she doesn't *appreciate* what he does.

Mistakes women commonly make	Why he doesn't feel loved
4. She corrects his behavior and tells him what to do, as if he were a child.	4. He feels unloved because he does not feel *admired*.
5. She expresses her upset feelings indirectly with rhetorical questions like, "How could you do that?"	5. He feels unloved because he feels she has taken away her *approval* of him. He no longer feels like the good guy.
6. When he makes decisions or takes initiatives she corrects or criticizes him.	6. He feels unloved because she does not *encourage* him to do things on his own.

Just as women easily make mistakes when they don't understand what men primarily need, men also make mistakes. Men generally don't recognize the ways they communicate that are disrespectful and unsupportive to women. A man may even know that she is unhappy with him, but unless he understands *why* she feels unloved and *what* she needs he cannot change his approach.

Through understanding a woman's primary needs, a man can be more sensitive to and respectful of her needs. The following is a list of communication mistakes men make in relation to a woman's primary emotional needs.

Mistakes men make	Why she doesn't feel loved
1. He doesn't listen, gets easily distracted, doesn't ask interested or concerned questions.	1. She feels unloved because he is not attentive or showing that he *cares*.
2. He takes her feelings literally and corrects her. He thinks she is asking for solutions so he gives advice.	2. She feels unloved because he doesn't *understand* her.

<u>Mistakes</u> <u>men</u> <u>make</u>	<u>Why</u> <u>she</u> <u>doesn't</u> <u>feel</u> <u>loved</u>
3. He listens but then gets angry and blames her for upsetting him or for bringing him down.	3. She feels unloved because he doesn't *respect* her feelings.
4. He minimizes the importance of her feelings and needs. He makes children or work more important.	4. She feels unloved because he is not *devoted* to her and doesn't honor her as special.
5. When she is upset, he explains why he is right and why she should not be upset.	5. She feels unloved because he doesn't *validate* her feelings but instead makes her feel wrong and unsupported.

Learning to Listen Without Getting Angry

The number one way a man can succeed in fulfilling a woman's primary love needs is through communication. As we have discussed before, communication is particularly important on Venus. By learning to listen to a woman's feelings, a man can effectively shower a woman with caring, understanding, respect, devotion, validation, and reassurance.

One of the biggest problems men have with listening to women is that they become frustrated or angry because they forget that women are from Venus and they are supposed to communicate differently. The chart below outlines some ways to remember these differences and makes some suggestions about what to do.

<u>What</u> <u>to</u> <u>remember</u>	<u>What</u> <u>to</u> <u>do</u> <u>and</u> <u>what</u> <u>not</u> <u>to</u> <u>do</u>
1. Remember anger comes from not understanding her point of view, and this is never her fault.	1. Take responsibility to understand. Don't blame her for upsetting you. Start again trying to understand.

What to remember	What to do and what not to do
2. Remember that feelings don't always make sense right away, but they're still valid and need empathy.	2. Breathe deeply, don't say anything! Relax and let go of trying to control. Try to imagine how you would feel if you saw the world through her eyes.
3. Remember that anger may come from not knowing what to do to make things better. Even if she doesn't immediately feel better, your listening and understanding are helping.	3. Don't blame her for not feeling better from your solutions. How can she feel better when solutions are not what she needs? Resist the urge to offer solutions.
4. Remember you don't have to agree to understand her point of view or to be appreciated as a good listener.	4. If you wish to express a differing point of view make sure she is finished and then rephrase her point of view before giving your own. Do not raise your voice.

When a man can listen to a woman's feelings without getting angry and frustrated, he gives her a wonderful gift. He makes it safe for her to express herself. The more she is able to express herself, the more she feels heard and understood, and the more she is able to give a man the loving trust, acceptance, appreciation, admiration, approval, and encouragement that he needs.

The Art of Empowering a Man

Just as men need to learn the art of listening to fulfill a woman's primary love needs, women need to learn the art of empowerment. When a woman enlists the support of a man, she empowers him to be all that he can be. A man feels empowered when he is trusted, accepted, appreciated, admired, approved of, and encouraged.

Like in our story of the knight in shining armor, many women try to help their man by improving him but unknowingly weaken or hurt him. Any attempt to change him takes away the loving trust, acceptance, appreciation, admiration, approval, and encouragement that are his primary needs.

The secret of empowering a man is never to try to change him or improve him. Certainly you may want him to change—just don't act on that desire. Only if he directly and specifically asks for advice is he open to assistance in changing.

Give Trust and Not Advice

On Venus, it is considered a loving gesture to offer advice. But on Mars it is not. Women need to remember that Martians do not offer advice unless it is directly requested. A way of showing love is to trust another Martian to solve his problems on his own.

This doesn't mean a woman has to squash her feelings. It's OK for her to feel frustrated or even angry, as long as she doesn't try to change him. Any attempt to change him is unsupportive and counterproductive.

When a woman loves a man, she often begins trying to improve their relationship. In her exuberance she makes him a target for her improvements. She begins a gradual process of slowly rehabilitating him.

Why Men Resist Change

In a myriad of ways she tries to change him or improve him. She thinks her attempts to change him are loving, but he feels controlled, manipulated, rejected, and unloved. He will stubbornly reject her because he feels she is rejecting him. When a woman tries to change a man, he is not getting the loving trust and acceptance he actually needs to change and grow.

When I ask a room filled with hundreds of women and men they all have had the same experience: The more a woman tries to change a man, the more he resists.

The problem is that when a man resists her attempts to improve him, she misinterprets his response. She mistakenly thinks he is not willing to change, probably because he does not love her enough. The truth is, however, that he is resistant to changing because he believes he is not being loved enough. When a man feels loved, trusted, accepted, appreciated, and so forth, automatically he begins to change, grow, and improve.

Two Kinds of Men/One Kind of Behavior

There are two kinds of men. One will become incredibly defensive and stubborn when a woman tries to change him, while the other will agree to change but later will forget and revert back to the old behavior. A man either actively resists or passively resists.

When a man does not feel loved just the way he is, he will either consciously or unconsciously repeat the behavior that is not being accepted. He feels an inner compulsion to repeat the behavior until he feels loved and accepted.

For a man to improve himself he needs to feel loved in an accepting way. Otherwise he defends himself and stays the same. He needs to feel accepted just the way he is, and then he, on his own, will look for ways to improve.

Men Don't Want to Be Improved

Just as men want to explain why women shouldn't be upset, women want to explain why men shouldn't behave the way they do. Just as men mistakenly want to "fix" women, women mistakenly try to "improve" men.

Men see the world through Martian eyes. Their motto is, "Don't fix it, if it isn't broken." When a woman attempts to change a man, he receives the message that she thinks he is broken. This hurts a man and makes him very defensive. He doesn't feel loved and accepted.

A man needs to be accepted regardless of his imperfections. To accept a person's imperfections is not easy, especially when we see how he could become better. It does, however, become easier when we understand that the best way to help him grow is to let go of *trying* to change him in any way.

The following chart lists ways a woman can support a man in growing and changing by giving up trying to change him in any way:

How to Give Up Trying to Change a Man

<u>What</u> <u>she</u> <u>needs</u> <u>to</u> <u>remember</u>	<u>What</u> <u>she</u> <u>can</u> <u>do</u>
1. Remember: don't ask him too many questions when he is upset or he will feel you are trying to change him.	1. Ignore that he is upset unless he wants to talk to you about it. Show some initial concern, but not too much, as an invitation to talk.
2. Remember: give up trying to improve him in any way. He needs your love, not rejection, to grow.	2. Trust him to grow on his own. Honestly share feelings but without the demand that he change.
3. Remember: when you offer unsolicited advice he may feel mistrusted, controlled, or rejected.	3. Practice patience and trust that he will learn on his own what he needs to learn. Wait until he asks for your advice.
4. Remember: when a man becomes stubborn and resists change he is not feeling loved; he is afraid to admit his mistakes for fear of not being loved.	4. Practice showing him that he doesn't have to be perfect to deserve your love. Practice forgiveness.
5. Remember: if you make sacrifices hoping he will do the same for you then he will feel pressured to change.	5. Practice doing things for yourself and not depending on him to make you happy.

As men and women learn to support each other in the ways that are most important for their own unique needs, change and growth will become automatic. With a greater awareness of your partner's six primary needs you can redirect your loving support according to their needs and make your relationships dramatically easier and more fulfilling.

3

New Skills for Listening and Learning

Masculine Skills for Listening Without Getting Upset

To give a woman the emotional support she requires, a man needs to listen in a new way, using new relationship skills. When she is upset, his most powerful means of assisting her in feeling better is to listen without getting upset that she is upset. To do this successfully, he does not have to make major changes in himself. Instead, he is required only to reconnect to his ancient warrior skills.

By learning to duck and dodge what he hears as blame, mistrust, and criticism, a man can gradually learn to listen patiently and not get shot to pieces. Through listening in a skillful manner so that he is not hurt by her words and feelings, he will begin to hear her calmly.

While he is perfectly capable of mastering this relationship skill, it is not as easy for him as women assume. His mate's conscious assistance in this process can greatly speed up his progress.

We have already discussed that hearing a woman talk about problems is particularly hard on a man because he either is inclined to offer solutions that she doesn't appreciate or feels blamed for what is bothering her.

If a man simply practices listening passively for more than ten minutes without clear guidelines, and without doing something to make his mate feel better or at least defend himself, he will become increasingly frustrated and upset.

Even if she does not intend to attack or blame him when she talks about her feelings, he may feel that she does. Merely listening is too inactive for him. It is as if he is standing in front of a firing squad. When she begins to talk, he wants to either fight back or put on a blindfold.

Instead of allowing himself to be wounded by his partner's words, a man can practice the new relationship skill of ducking and dodging. When he feels under attack, he can actively support her by not taking it personally. He is superbly equipped to do this because protecting himself from harm is the most basic of warrior skills. If he has survived this long, with a few adjustments he can begin applying his skills in conversation.

Emotional Self-Defense

The instincts that sent warriors boldly into battle to defend themselves and protect their loved ones come into play when a modern man tries to listen to a modern woman. To prevail, he must learn to duck and dodge.

Ducking and dodging require new mental strategies for correctly interpreting the situation. Instead of reacting to blame and criticism, a man learns to hear the correct loving message in her words and responds in ways that diminish friction and conflict. Ducking and dodging allow a man to keep his cool and respond respectfully to a woman's need to communicate.

When he listens to a woman *without* ducking and dodging, he will be repeatedly assaulted by her words and begin to feel blamed, criticized, unacknowledged, misunderstood, rejected, mistrusted, or unappreciated. No matter how much he loves her, after about three direct hits he will no longer be capable of listening to her in a supportive way. War breaks out.

When a man is struck by a woman's words, it is much harder to restrain his ancient warrior instincts to intimidate, threaten, or retaliate. Once these defensive responses are triggered, he will attempt either to change her mind through arguing or protect her from his own aggressive reactions by emotionally withdrawing. However, through new relationship skills of listening without getting struck, he can easily sidestep provocative reactions.

Women Still Want to Be Protected

Although modern women are independent and assertive, their female natures still seek out strong men who can provide protection. They still want to be protected, but in a different sense.

Women now look to men to provide the emotional climate in which they can safely explore and express their feelings. When a man can listen to a woman's feelings and allow her to articulate them without responding negatively, she is not only very appreciative but more attracted to him as a result.

Through ducking and dodging, a man will avoid getting upset along with his partner and will create a new dimension of protection for the woman he loves. This new ability and strength not only helps her but ensures that he too will get the love he deserves.

Security is the most important gift a contemporary man can give a woman. In hunter/nurturer societies, that security was primarily physical. Today, it is emotional as well.

The Importance of Safety

When a man seeks an intimate partner, he wants primarily to be needed and appreciated. When a woman seeks a mate, a man's ability to protect her is a key job requirement. This is a very primal feeling directly connected to her emotional well-being.

Down through the centuries, women have looked to men for protection because it was crucial to their family's survival. This protector role carries over into our generation of relationships, but now, as we've said, it is more linked to emotional security. It means that she can talk without worrying about hurting him and without reprisal. It means that she can be in a bad mood without her mate's holding it against her or ignoring her.

The Emotional Freedom to Be Herself

Women are under such constant pressure to be loving and sweet that the freedom to be themselves is the greatest gift a man can give them. Even if he doesn't really understand her feelings, the attempt to do so calmly makes her feel powerfully supported.

Sometimes a woman doesn't understand her own feelings until she freely talks about them. If she doesn't have to worry about her man's losing control or withdrawing his love, she is doubly relieved and deeply grateful. Even if she remains upset *with him* after receiving this support, it becomes much easier for her to draw deep from her loving center the strength to forgive and forget.

Women Don't Demand Agreement

Men don't realize that an emotionally upset woman is not demanding agreement or submission from him. She just wants to be considered. He mistakenly assumes that he has to fight to be himself when she only wants to feel heard, not stop him or control him.

A man does not instinctively understand this because he is so much more goal-oriented.

When a woman is upset, she first wants to talk about it and decide later what she thinks should happen. A man mistakenly assumes that he has to give in to her feelings and sacrifice if he wants to please her. He mistakenly concludes that he has to agree with her point of view before she can feel OK again. If he doesn't agree and doesn't want to give in, he feels driven to point out the deficiencies in her argument to get her to agree with him.

Through understanding this difference, a man can contain his tendency to argue when a woman is emotional. When I use my brains instead of my guts, I can easily duck and dodge. This does not mean that I should disregard my gut reactions. They are inevitable. What is required in a relationship is that men control their instincts when they are feeling blamed or attacked and not retaliate.

Certainly there will be times when a man is struck by her words and gets upset. It's only to be expected. A woman can handle a man being upset if he can contain his negative reactions and respond respectfully. As long as he contains his feelings and doesn't lose control by dumping them on her, it counts as support. However, one loose derogatory zinger can undo twenty minutes of attentive support.

When emotions are involved, it is important for men to think before they act. Whenever I contain my reactions and use my brain to respond, both Bonnie and I win. Otherwise, we both lose. I may win the argument, but I will eventually lose her trust.

What Women Admire in Men

A woman admires a man if he has the strength to control his emotions and the sensitivity to consider the merits and validity of what she is saying. He doesn't have to put his tail between his legs and do whatever she wants.

Women are turned off by passive and submissive men. They don't want to be the boss in an intimate relationship. They want to be equal partners. If a man respects a woman's primary need to be heard, she will respond by becoming equally respectful of his wishes.

Why Men Argue with Feelings

Men assume that an emotional woman is inflexible in her thinking. They don't realize that at such a time, when a woman talks about her feelings she is not making conclusions or expressing fixed opinions. When a woman shares negative emotions, she is generally in the middle of the process of discovering what she feels to be true. She is not stating an objective fact.

She talks to "discover" the range of feelings within herself—not to give an accurate description of objective reality. That's what men do. Instead, she is more concerned with discovering and describing what is going on in her subjective, inner world.

Meanwhile, I'm waiting for Bonnie to answer my question about what *she* feels we should buy instead of the computer, but she's still in the midst of discovering what her feelings are. Finally, she tells me, "It's not that I have this all thought out. It's just a feeling. I feel like you get exactly what you want and I get seconds. Maybe I'm mad that you want so much more than I do. When I want something, it doesn't seem so earthshaking."

I realize that "It's not that I have this all thought out" means she's still talking feelings, not facts. But even with her help, I'm still struggling to dodge and duck from feeling criticized and unappreciated. Inwardly, I'm fuming.

How can you say you get seconds? I silently demand. I do so many things for you. I work hard so that you can have practically anything you want. How do you have the nerve to even suggest you're not important to me! Although these are my true gut reactions, I thoroughly appreciate how counterproductive it would be to express them.

If I were to "tell her what I think of her," it would only be to try to convince her that she is wrong or is being very unfair. I would succeed only in invalidating her feelings and confirming her doubts and mistrust. But by listening without attacking her, I am giving her the time and opportunity to talk more, remember the good things about me, and let go of the negative comments *on her own*. Despite my resentment, I'm convinced that she soon will.

When a woman has a chance to share her feelings freely, she begins to feel more loving. Sometimes she may realize how wrong, incorrect, or unfair her statements sounded, but in most cases she just forgets them as she begins to see things from a more loving perspective.

It's hard for men to relate readily to this mood change because it's foreign to their natures and they just can't fathom it. When a man is upset and talks with the person who is upsetting him, he tends to remain upset unless that person agrees with him in some significant way or until he can find a solution. Simply listening to him and nodding your head in sympathy is not enough if he is really upset.

After a woman shares a negative feeling, a man mistakenly takes it as her "final" conclusion and thinks she is blaming him. He doesn't know that her feelings will change if he just lets her talk them out.

Why Men Feel Blamed

Quite commonly in counseling, a woman will share her feelings and a man will feel attacked and blamed. This is how it goes:

He says: "You're blaming me."
She says: "No I'm not. I'm only sharing my feelings."
He then says: "But your feelings tell me you *are* blaming me. When you say you feel ignored, you're saying I'm not attentive. When you say you don't feel loved, you're accusing me."
She then says: "No I'm not. I'm just talking about how *I* feel. I am not saying something about *you*."
He says: "Yes you are! I'm the only one you are married to."
She says: "I can't talk to you."
He says: "There you go again blaming me for how you feel."

Without some intervention, they will go on arguing until they give up in frustration.

Men must understand what is really going on inside a woman when she sounds blaming. On the flip side, a woman can make communication much easier by appreciating why her partner imagines that she is blaming him.

As men begin to comprehend the female thinking and feeling process, they will see that from the woman's viewpoint, she really isn't blaming them.

For years I couldn't comprehend this when I was listening to my wife. It was really hard to dodge when I felt repeatedly blamed. While she shared her feelings, I would feel an urgent need to argue with her. Then one day all that changed. It was a realization that occurred while I accompanied her on a little shopping excursion.

As I observed my wife shopping, I noticed a striking difference between us. When I shopped, I found what I wanted, bought it, and got out as quickly as possible, like a hunter making a kill and hurrying home with it. Bonnie, however, was very happy trying on many outfits.

When she finally settled on a shop that interested her, I was relieved and parked myself in a chair by the dressing room. She was very excited about several outfits. I was very excited because not only would she be happy but we could finally leave. How wrong I was!

Instead of simply buying an outfit or two quickly, she took what seemed like years trying on each one to get a feel for it. As she preened in the mirror, she made comments like, "This one's sort of cute, isn't it? I'm not sure though. Is it really me? The colors are good. I really love the length."

Finally she announced, "No, it's not me." This scene was repeated with outfit after outfit. Sometimes before changing out of one, she would say firmly, "I like this one."

After forty-five minutes of this, we left without her buying anything. To my surprise, she wasn't the least bit frustrated. I could not ever imagine putting that much time and energy into the hunt, coming home empty-handed, and still being happy.

How to Dodge Blame

As I reflected on that incident, I realized that this was the key to understanding why a woman sounds blaming when she claims she is not.

You see, an overwhelmed woman talks about her feelings the way she shops. She is not expecting you to buy a particular feeling any more than she is necessarily going to buy it herself. She is basically trying on emotional outfits to see if they fit. Just because she takes a lot of time trying on an outfit or testing an emotion doesn't mean it's "her."

Now, in the spirit of fairness, when my wife seems to blame me I pretend that we're shopping and she is just beginning to try things on. It may be an hour before we actually "leave the store," but only then can I know what she finally believes.

Negative Feelings Are Not Permanent

It is easier to dodge a woman's resistant feelings and not feel blamed if a man remembers that her feelings are not permanent and that she is just trying them on for size. If he argues with her, she will become defensive. Having to protect herself prevents her from getting immediately to the place where she can return her negative feelings to the rack and "buy" more positive ones.

Women speak negatives out loud to discover the positive, loving, and more accurate picture of what happened. Even if some mistake was made by the man, as she lets go of negative feelings, she is able to see the bigger picture and remember all the good he does as well.

Articulating negatives help women accept men and love them

just the way they are without expecting or even depending on them to be perfect. To find real love that does not demand perfection, a woman needs a man's support so that she can express her feelings without being held accountable for every word she utters.

Feelings Are Not Facts

When a man expresses a feeling, it is more like a fact—something he believes to be true but doesn't have a lot of objective evidence to back up. This is not what a woman means when she shares her feelings. For women, feelings are much less about the outer world and more about their *experience* of the outer world. For women, feelings and facts are very different animals.

How to Duck Criticism

A man needs to remember that all feelings are temporary. By listening to a woman's negative emotions, he allows her the opportunity to discover her positive feelings as well. In return, a woman can help *him* duck and dodge by making supportive comments. These comments we will explore more thoroughly in the next chapter.

Feelings Change

Another tip for successful dodging is to remember that negative feelings can shift 180 degrees in just a few minutes without a man's saying anything. If a man reacts in a negative way to a woman's negative feelings, she doesn't feel understood and must continue explaining those feelings before she can move on. Reacting in a negative way only prolongs the process.

It is not a contradiction—in fact, it's perfectly normal—for a woman to say in a single conversation, "I feel like you only care about yourself," *and* "You really are a very caring person, you give me so much support."

Once aware of a woman's inherent flexibility, a man can relax and listen instead of focusing on how to change her mind. When a man doesn't know how to dodge, he resists by "spilling his guts," which in turn forces a woman to lose her flexibility and become closed, rigid, and righteous.

Disarming by Asking More Questions

Whenever a man asks a woman questions, he sends her the *disarming* and soothing message that he cares and that he is there for her. By asking questions or making statements like, "How can I help you?" or "Tell me more," he releases her from feeling she's fighting an uphill battle.

The secret of supporting a woman who feels upset or overwhelmed is to help her work through her feelings by getting her to speak more words—negative or positive, accurate or inaccurate, defensive or vulnerable. The more words he can hear and dodge, the more she will feel heard and seen, which will shift her attitude back toward love.

Bottom-Line Advice for Men to Support a Woman

Remember, if a woman doesn't have to focus on getting a man to listen to her, she can do what is most natural for her—talking and shifting her *own* attitude. To support her in feeling more loving and accepting, here is some bottom-line advice for men:

1. When you suspect she is upset, don't wait for her to initiate the conversation (when you initiate, it takes away 50 percent of her emotional charge).
2. As you let her talk, keep reminding yourself that it doesn't help to get upset with her for being upset.
3. Whenever you feel an urgent need to interrupt or correct, don't.
4. When you don't know what to say, say nothing. If you can't say something positive or respectful, keep quiet.
5. If she won't talk, ask more questions until she does.
6. Whatever you do, don't correct or judge her feelings.
7. Remain as calm and centered as possible, and keep a lock on your strong reactions. (If you lose control and "spill your guts" even for a moment, you lose and have to start all over at a disadvantage.)

Just as ducking, dodging, and disarming are all fighting skills, so also is delivering. In a real fight, a man needs to wait and watch for the right moment to deliver his punch and make contact. In a loving conversation, a man needs to apply this same skill. He needs to watch and wait for the right moment to deliver a word or phrase of support that will end the battle.

The Importance of Eye Contact

When women are upset, they want to be seen. Unlike men, they don't want to be ignored or left alone. The most important thing a man can do is to notice when his partner is upset. When she feels seen, she can more directly see herself and more efficiently explore her feelings.

When a man listens, his basic tendency is to look away in order to think about what is being said. It is hard for women to understand this difference because when they talk about their feelings with each other, they instinctively deliver their support by lots of eye contact.

If a man simply stares into a woman's eyes when she talks about feelings, his mind will start to go blank and he will space out. Without understanding that a woman needs more eye contact than he does, a man tends to look away to figure out what his partner means or how he is going to respond.

Learning to maintain eye contact not only delivers a very important kind of support but also helps a man to check his reaction to attempt immediately to offer a solution to her problems. The trick for a man is not only to remember to do it, but to do it without going blank.

This can be accomplished if he looks in a special way. Instead of staring, he should first look in her eyes for two to three seconds. Then, when he would naturally turn his head and look away, he should instead look to the tip of her nose. After that, he should look at her lips, then her chin, and then her whole face. Then he should start over.

This procedure keeps him looking in her direction and yet frees him from spacing out or going blank. It can also be relaxing because it is something else he can do instead of passively doing nothing.

Cold Fronts

When I notice a cold front coming from my wife's direction, my old approach to making her feel better was to assume that she needed space to be alone. After a while I would notice that it was getting colder and colder, and the chill was definitely directed toward me. I would grumble to myself that I didn't deserve Bonnie's cold shoulder and inwardly begin getting furious. Eventually we would negatively interact and sparks would fly.

Once I understood more about women, I no longer sat

around ignoring my wife when she was cold and getting angrier as she grew more distant.

It eventually occurred to me that by giving her more space, I was only making things worse. I finally realized that Bonnie didn't want more space but wanted more contact and attention. Most of the time when I was feeling the cold front, it was not even about me—she just needed to talk in order to warm up. But when I didn't notice and come over to touch her and ask questions in a caring manner, it just made her more cold and distant. So, even though her feelings weren't initially about me, they soon became so.

Now I cope with cold fronts by preparing myself to put on a warm jacket and fly straight into the storm. By touching her and initiating a conversation, I know she will eventually warm up to me without my having to do anything else but dodge, duck, disarm, and deliver.

How to Warm Up a Cold Woman

Now when I sense a coldness coming from Bonnie, I immediately go up and touch her.

If she doesn't pull back when I make physical contact, I know that her distress is not about me. If she does pull back, I realize that I'm going to need to duck and dodge a lot more, but I also know she'll get back to loving me even more.

I touch not only to defuse her anger, but also to check the temperature. If she is really angry with me, I find out and ask the appropriate questions. If she isn't, I simply relax from needing to duck and dodge. To initiate conversation, I ask her how her day was or if she's upset with me.

In most cases, a woman will respond to these questions with, "Oh, it's not you. There is just so much going on," and will then continue to talk. Even if she *was* a little upset with her mate, she will quickly tend to dismiss those feelings because he's initiated the conversation. When she feels supported, she can be very generous with her love.

What to Do When She Is Angry with Him

When a woman is angry with a man, the most powerful message he can send her is that she has a right to be angry, that it is safe for her to be angry, and that he wants to understand what he did to upset her so that he can stop doing it.

When I touch Bonnie and she remains cold or pulls away, the most important thing for me to remember is not to be hurt or offended by her rejection. Since I'm testing the temperature, I am prepared for a possible rejection. If I were not prepared, I would instinctually react with anger.

Let's look at another example. One day I was feeling a cold front that had been building for several hours. I truly had no idea what it was about. The old me would have reacted by feeling unappreciated and unfairly denied. Instead, I knew how to quickly nip it in the bud by giving her a chance to talk about it.

When I touched her, she immediately pulled away. But instead of stalking off, I summoned up my relationship skills and didn't take her action personally. I continued to stand there, and look in her direction, wondering what was bothering her. As it worked out, it took at least fifteen to thirty seconds for her to even realize that she had rejected me. Since I didn't react negatively, it was easy to rebuild trust.

I now knew for certain that she was angry with me. To protect myself from feeling hurt by her anger and blame, I was careful not to ask a question like, "Are you upset with me?" or "Did I do something wrong?" To protect myself from getting hurt, it was best to at least start out with a question that didn't directly link me to her anger.

The Power of Gentle Persistence

The most effective neutral question to ask at times like this is: "Do you want to talk about something?" If the answer is no, it is easy to dodge because deep inside I can easily understand her not wanting to talk.

I say, "I really want to understand what happened." Again I am careful not to open myself up to much of her anger.

She pauses and says, "There's not much to say." That tells me that there is a lot to say. I begin preparing myself to duck and dodge.

My objective is to gently persist in my goal of being there for her. By holding my ground without demanding more, I earn her respect, and she gets the message that I really care.

Bearing that in mind, I say, "Is it something I said or did?"

Her response is a deep inhalation and a long sigh, indicating that she really doesn't want to talk about it.

I say, "If it is, I really want to know," then, after pausing, "If I hurt you, I want to know what I did so that I won't do it again."

At this point she opens up and gently replies, "The other day when we were talking, you answered the phone right in the middle of what I was saying. Afterward, you didn't even ask me to finish the thought. I felt really hurt."

I say, "I'm sorry, that was insensitive of me." Although a surge of explanations come up, I quickly push them away and reach out to touch her shoulder. This time she receives it.

Bonnie proceeds to talk about her feelings, and after a while we feel very close again. I would never have known how to do this years ago. How could I? Nobody ever taught me. But now that I am "working" according to a new job description based on new relationship skills, I know better.

What It Takes to Duck and Dodge

Once you've mastered the elements of these new relationship skills, it only takes a few moments to discern how to use them. It's similar to hitting a tennis ball or golf ball—a lot of practice goes into developing the swing, but once learned, it's practically automatic.

Learning to listen is similar to learning any new skill. When you first drive a stick shift, for example, the mechanism seems very complex. After practice, though, a seasoned driver doesn't even think about shifting because the process becomes a series of reflex actions.

For a man, learning to listen attentively without getting upset or frustrated when a woman is upset is definitely a new and difficult skill. However, with a lot of practice it can easily become second nature.

Feminine Skills for Talking So a Man Will Listen

When women address men as they have always talked to other women, men either don't get it or just stop listening. It is as if women were speaking a different language that men tend to misunderstand. A woman can greatly assist a man in learning her language by making a few small but significant changes in her communication style.

By learning to pause and prepare a man before sharing her feelings, a woman immediately begins getting the kind of support she most needs.

This formula for talking so that a man will listen can be as simple as saying the following phrase: "You don't have to say anything or do anything, I just need to talk about my feelings in order to feel better."

Through first pausing and then preparing him in this way, he doesn't feel an obligation to offer suggestions or think up solutions to make her feel better. Instead of focusing on attempting to solve her problems while she is talking, he can relax and really listen. By doing less, he can actually give her the emotional support she is really looking for.

Talking in a logical and focused manner is primarily how men communicate and business is done. For eight hours each day to varying degrees, a working woman is required to express herself in this way. If she limits herself to talking "Male," a man may listen more, but it pulls her away from her femininity.

When a woman gets home, her first priority is finding the balance to be feminine again. However, if she abruptly begins talking "Female" and tries to share her feelings without clear guidelines, it will inevitably ruin her intimate relationships. Eventually, she will either give up on men or close down the feminine part of her that needs to talk. Both such courses are disastrous to her happiness and fulfillment.

To relax and connect back to her warm, loving, feminine feelings after being combative, competitive, efficient, and goal-oriented during the day, a woman needs the freedom, permission, and support in her relationships to communicate her feelings in a non-goal-oriented, nonlogical, nonaccurate, and nonrational way.

To recuperate from her day, she needs to freely expand through expressing her feelings. If she is always editing them to make sure they are correct, accurate, and presented in a logical manner, she stays in her male side. Without understanding what a woman requires to nurture her female side, men become overly frustrated with a woman's need to talk in a feminine way.

A man does not instinctively know this because his male side is nurtured when he talks in a focused, direct, clear, logical, and goal-oriented manner after a lot of silent thought, consideration, and deliberation. He doesn't realize that to demand this focused approach from his partner is counterproductive and will inevitably prevent her from being feminine.

A New Dilemma

The contemporary woman is faced with a new dilemma. Either she trains herself to talk like a man and loses a part of herself as well as an essential source of happiness, or she disregards a man's resistance and lets it loose. In response to her free expression of feelings, he stops listening, and she eventually loses his love and support. Since neither approach works, it's fortunate that there is another way.

Traditionally, women didn't depend on men for nurturing conversations, nor were they required to talk like men throughout the day. If a woman had to be more linear when she occasionally talked with a man, it was OK because she had the whole day to talk in an expanded female style.

The need to communicate with men is a new challenge for both women and men. By applying new feminine skills, a woman can greatly assist a man in listening to her feelings. Once a man is prepared, a woman can relax and let go. This is the secret. By her saying a few words, a man can be conditioned to effectively deal with her different style of communicating. Even if her words would normally sound critical and blaming to a man in "Male" language, even if he is not yet good at ducking and dodging, if he is prepared correctly he can even handle a direct hit.

The Great Houdini

My favorite example of a man's need to be prepared comes from the life of the great Houdini.

The magician Harry Houdini offered the challenge that he could get out of anything. He was an escape artist. He became famous for getting out of chained boxes, straitjackets, bank safes, and jails. The second challenge he made is less well known.

He made the challenge that anyone, no matter how big they

were, could punch him in the stomach and he wouldn't be hurt by it. He could take any punch.

One Halloween night during the intermission of his magic show, a young college student came backstage and asked, "Is it true that you can take any punch?"

Houdini said, "Yes."

Before Houdini had a chance to prepare himself, the student gave him a quick jab. It was that quick punch that killed the great Houdini. He was rushed to the hospital but died the next day.

Like Houdini, a man can handle a woman's verbal punches if he is prepared and can, in a sense, tighten his stomach muscles so that he doesn't get hurt. If he is not prepared, then he is overly vulnerable and can easily be hurt.

There are a variety of ways in which a woman can prepare a man so that he can hear what she is saying without getting bruised. In this chapter I will suggest some that may be appropriate for you and some that may not be. As time passes, other ways of preparing may feel more appropriate as you and your mate grow into them.

Trying on Different Outfits

Treat these suggestions as if they were different outfits that you might like to wear. Try them, see if they fit, and if you like them, then check them out with your partner to see if your partner likes them as well. Take your pick.

I suggest the following examples as a springboard for developing other expressions as well. Once you get the hang of it, it will become a natural way of supporting the person you love most in your life. Eventually you will find yourself integrating these advanced relationship skills into all your relationships.

Giving a Man His Job Description

When a woman talks, a man commonly does not know what is required of him. Listening is difficult for him because he misunderstands what is expected or what she is really saying in her language. If he is not skilled in ducking and dodging, the more he *cares,* the more he will feel hit by what sounds like criticism in "male talk."

A woman's new task is to casually let him know what she needs before she begins to talk. By clearly giving him a job description in a language that he can understand, he can relax and not exert himself in trying to figure out what she wants. This is a new twist for a woman, but once learned it frees her to express her power as a woman in a new way.

Using Old Skills in a New Way

Although it has a new twist, "preparing" is really an ancient feminine skill at which women are very adept. Their instinctive nature demands that they prepare. While cavemen focused on the day's hunt, cavewomen prepared for the future.

There is an intuitive knowledge in women that understands that everything grows naturally in small steps when the right conditions are created and patiently nurtured. Her instinctive motto is: An ounce of prevention is worth a pound of cure.

Until now, a woman's traditional daily responsibilities reflected this tendency to prepare. Each day she would think ahead to plan and prepare meals for her family. To create a nurturing setting for herself and the family, she would prepare the home to make it as beautiful and uplifting as possible. To grow a garden, she would first prepare the ground before planting the seeds.

As mothers, women have always taken the time to prepare their children for the world, step by step. In guiding a child to play independently, a mother will first set up the appropriate toys or set the conditions. To prepare the child to read, *she* will read to the child. Through "preparing" a nurturing setting she knows that the child will automatically grow and flourish.

Traditionally, women put much more attention in how they dress and appear. When a women gets dressed, she instinctively takes more time to prepare so that her personal expression is appropriate to the event or setting. Preparing her face with the right makeup, preparing her skin because it is more sensitive, and wearing ornaments on her body to attract the appropriate attention are all expressions of this tendency to prepare.

Women are always preparing. It is their nature, and they are good at it. One of their great hidden frustrations is that they do not know how to prepare a man to listen. Without a clear understanding of how men speak "Male" and not "Female," a woman cannot intuit the necessity of preparing to have a conversation. She naively assumes that if he loves her, he will instinctively understand her language.

Even so, women do prepare a man to listen but generally in instinctive ways that would work with other women but not with men. She mistakenly assumes that if she asks him lots of questions about his day, he will be prepared to listen to her. This kind of preparing doesn't work.

Preparing a man to listen is a new skill for women.

Times have changed so that even a well-meaning, intelligent man doesn't know what a woman really needs. While she talks, he will consistently offer a string of comments, corrections, and solutions. In response, she will say, "You don't understand."

Misunderstanding is one of the most common complaints women have about men. It is so worn that when a man hears it, he immediately gets defensive, because in "Male," she is saying that he is stupid and thus incapable of helping her.

This phrase "You don't understand" is so automatic to a woman that she has no idea that she is preventing a man from giving her the support she needs. Not only does this phrase sound like criticism, but it doesn't make any sense to him.

He feels that what he is doing demonstrates that he does understand what she is saying, and to maintain his pride he is willing to fight to prove it. Although he started out to help, he ends up wanting to argue.

How to Get a Man to Listen

When a woman says, "You don't understand," she really means, "You don't understand that right now I *don't* need a solution."

He, however, hears that she doesn't appreciate his solution and then gets hooked into arguing about the validity of his approach and explaining himself at a time when she only needs to talk.

However, here's an alternative. First, pause and consider that he is doing his best to understand and then say, "Let me try saying that in a different way."

When a man hears this phrase, it also conveys the message that the man has not fully understood her, but in a noncritical way. He is much more willing to listen and reconsider what she is saying. He does not feel criticized or blamed, and as a result is more eager to support her. Without understanding what makes men tick, it would be nearly impossible for a woman to figure out that a man would greatly prefer to hear, "Let me try saying this in a different way" to "You don't understand." To a man, however, the difference is so obvious that he would never think to suggest it.

The Wisdom of Pausing and Preparing

When a man is offering solutions and a woman wants just to be heard, advanced relationship skills are available that do not offend him, through which she can assist him in giving her the support she wants. By learning how to "pause" and then "prepare" him to listen she can continue without getting interrupted by his solutions.

The sooner a woman makes it clear that she doesn't need a solution, the easier it will be for her mate to shift gears from the "fixing" mode to the "hearing mode." For example, if a man has been listening and offering solutions for twenty minutes and the woman then pauses to let him know that she doesn't need his solutions, he will feel foolish, unappreciated, and defensive.

Sometimes, when my wife, Bonnie, is talking about her problems, I begin offering little solutions. Even though I teach new relationship skills, I sometimes forget to duck and dodge.

Instead of expressing an immediate reaction like, "You don't understand" or "You're not listening," she pauses and prepares me to support her. Instead of focusing on what I am doing wrong, she just reminds me of what I am supposed to be doing. This strategy is definitely a new relationship skill.

She says in a very casual, matter-of-fact way, "Oh, you don't have to solve this, I just need to talk about it. I'm already starting to feel better. I think I just need to feel heard."

She does this in the same tone of voice as one might use with a dinner guest who after dinner starts washing the dishes. In that situation a gracious host would automatically say, "Oh, you don't have to bother cleaning up, I'll get to it later. It's no big deal. Let's just go in the living room."

When she gently reminds me in this way of my new job requirements, I am very happy to make the shift to support her more. When a woman uses this kind of casual tone when she reminds a man, she thereby minimizes his mistake and allows him to easily continue listening.

Helping a Man to Listen

Once, after listening to Bonnie for about ten minutes, I began to look pretty beat-up. When I first came home I felt wonderful, but after hearing her complain about her life for ten minutes, I felt like a complete failure. I also felt "bummed out" because I thought she was really unhappy and that there was little I could do to change it.

She eventually noticed how down I appeared and told me, "You look the way I felt."

This was a revelation for me, because I had no idea that she was feeling better.

"You mean you felt this way, but you don't anymore?" I asked.

She said, "Yes, I feel much better now. I'm sorry you had to get bummed out, but I do feel much better."

I too suddenly felt much better. I told her, "Well, if you feel better, then I guess I do too. I thought we were destined to have a really awful evening."

I think that on an emotional level I was feeling we were destined to have an awful life. Bonnie's giving me a little positive feedback about how helpful my listening had been completely changed my mood.

Consequently, the next time we talked it was dramatically easier for me to listen without feeling defeated. Each time we talked *and* I experienced that she was happier as a result, it became easier the next time.

Helping Her to Pause with Reality Checks

I remember another time when Bonnie seemed really upset with me and said things like, "I feel like you never spend time with me anymore. Your work is more important than me. We used to be so much happier. I feel like things are just getting worse." These were hard words to hear, but I just kept ducking and dodging. I remembered that she was not talking about me but was just exploring what was really upsetting her.

At a certain point, in order to avoid feeling hit and getting even more upset, I helped her to pause by making a reality check. I said, "It's starting to sound like I do nothing right. Is there anything that has gotten better? Do I do anything right?"

In that moment she said, "Oh, yes, in the past I would never have been able to talk like this. I feel so much safer with you. I just need to get this out, and then I will feel so much better. I know this is hard for you, and I really appreciate it."

I said, "OK, tell me more." All I needed was to be reminded that her feelings were not directed at me as criticism.

One time she paused in the middle of a feeling conversation and said, "I know these feelings sound really unfair, I just need to express them and then I can easily let go of them. OK?"

Instantly I was able to relax and listen without feeling defensive. I said, "Thanks. Sounds good to me." It made a world of difference because she took a moment to pause and prepare me to listen.

It Sounds Worse Than It Is

Another time in the middle of a difficult conversation she said, "I know this must be hard for you. I just need to talk about it. It sounds a lot worse than it is. It really isn't a big deal to me. I just want you to know what goes on inside me."

Those words, "It sounds a lot worse than it is," or "It really isn't a big deal," were like honey to a bee. Although a man should never say to a woman, "It's not such a big deal," if a woman feels safe to share her feelings, and if she feels that he makes her feelings a big deal, then she can comfortably say, "It's not such a big deal."

For many women, this saying of "It's not such a big deal" would be counterproductive, particularly if while growing up they repeatedly got the message that their feelings were not a big deal. However, as an adult, when she experiences her feelings being respected and considered, then it becomes easier to make the kind of comments that assist a man in listening.

As a woman begins to understand men she realizes that a man will make her feelings much more important if she doesn't demand it. By preparing a man by saying, "It's not really a big deal. I just want you to consider how I feel," he will listen much more attentively than before.

At other times when a woman wants to initiate conversation, a good technique to use to prepare the man to listen is to say "I have a lot of feelings coming up, and I would like to talk about them. I just want you to know in advance that it sounds worse than it is. I just need to talk for a while and feel that you care. You don't have to say anything or do anything differently." This kind of approach will actually motivate him to think about how he might make changes to support you more.

What to Say When He Resists Listening

When a woman senses in advance that a man is going to resist what she is about to say, there are new ways to prepare him so that he can more easily duck and dodge. One woman told me that she just says to her husband, "Thanks for helping me here, I really appreciate your trying to duck and dodge what I'm saying. I know it must be hard to hear."

This is a great advanced relationship skills technique because many times, once a man is acknowledged for doing something difficult, he is happy to accept the job. A woman commonly takes for granted that a man should listen if he loves her. She doesn't instinctively understand how difficult it is for him to hear negative feedback from the person he cares most about. The expectation that he should easily hear and understand her because he loves her actually makes it harder for him to listen. When, however, she begins to acknowledge the difficulty, he is much more willing to do what it takes to listen.

At work, a man is happy to do a difficult job if he is paid accordingly. If, however, he is asked to take on a more difficult task and is not acknowledged or compensated for it, he begins to feel taken for granted, and as a result resists doing more. Likewise in a relationship, if a man is required to do something difficult, he wants his efforts to be appreciated; otherwise he may feel, "Why bother?"

You Don't Have to Change Your Mind

I remember once my stepdaughter Julie skillfully using a new communication technique when she was sixteen years old. I was very impressed. Bonnie and I had decided to take a three-day vacation while some work was being done on our house. For various reasons, Julie didn't want to go, but she also didn't want to stay in the middle of remodeling.

She said to me, "I have a lot of stay-home feelings about this and would like you just to listen. You don't have to change your mind, I just want you to consider my point of view." She then proceeded to tell me that she didn't like remodeling and wished we would do it in the future at a time when she could also be away from the house. As she shared her feelings, she became more emotional about it and then felt much better. I remember how much easier it was to hear her feelings because she had simply prepared me with the statement "You don't have to change your mind."

That one phrase set me free to listen. The result of that conversation was that in the future I was much more sensitive to her requests and made sure that we never left her at home with the remodeling again. It also made me more considerate in general.

This is the amazing thing about men. If they are approached in the wrong way, they get defensive and push away a woman's feelings and needs. Yet, in a positive sense, when a man is prepared in a way that helps him to be supportive, he is then much more considerate in general about everything.

It's Not Your Fault

The more a woman practices preparing a man, the less she will need to prepare him in the future. Each successful interaction assists a man in ducking and dodging more effectively the next time. As with the acquisition of any new skill, it is wise to begin with easy problems and then graduate to difficult ones. A woman's start-up assistance makes it easier for a man.

Just as men need assistance in learning to duck and dodge, so women sometimes forget to pause and prepare. At such times a woman must remember that it is never too late to correct things. If she notices that her man is having a hard time or is getting frustrated or angry, she can apply some pausing and preparing techniques.

She could say, "It makes sense to me that you feel. . . ." These words are validating to him and will help him cool off. Another major reason men get upset when listening is that they feel blamed. To help him dodge, just a few words can make a world of difference. I remember many conversations with Bonnie when she just said a few words and it allowed me to relax and listen instead of defend and fight.

Right in the middle of a conversation, when she sensed that I was getting bruised by her words, she paused and said, "I know this is probably sounding like blame. I don't want to blame you. You don't deserve that. I just need to talk about these feelings. I know there is another side to this. Let me first work through my feelings and then I will be able to appreciate your side of it."

After a few minutes, she started saying things like, "I can see that you really didn't mean. . . . I just misunderstood because I thought. . . . I really appreciate your not getting too upset about this."

When she finished, I really didn't need to say much in my own defense. I just said, "Well, I understand why you were upset, and I am glad we had this conversation." Even though at a gut level I hated having to listen to what sounded like blame, from a heart and head level of my being I knew that conversations like this were an important part of keeping the passion alive in a relationship.

You Don't Have to Say Anything

Probably the most potent and powerful phrase a woman can say to prepare a man to listen is: "You don't have to say anything." This message is important because it lets a man off the hook of needing to defend himself. In addition, it gently reminds him that he doesn't have to solve her problems.

A woman would generally not think of this because with other women it would be rude to say, "You don't have to say anything." When one woman talks in "Female," tradition commands that it will next be the other person's turn to talk; the unspoken agreement is that if I listen to you talk for five minutes, you must listen to me for five minutes.

With a man it is different. If she says, "You don't have to say anything," it is not rude—quite the contrary, he will be relieved. It is an easy job description.

You're Not Listening

Another common expression women use that is a complete turn-off for men is: "You're not listening." When a woman uses this phrase, it frustrates a man because he usually *is* listening in some way, or at least trying to. Even if he wasn't, it is hard for him to hear it because in childhood it was used repeatedly by his mother when she was upset with him.

Hearing it in adulthood, a man feels as if his mate is talking down to him and treating him like a child. He hears it as not only "degrading" but very "controlling." Just as a woman doesn't want to mother a man, a man does not want to be mothered. He feels she is blaming him when she is really just trying to be heard.

When a woman says, "You're not listening," it is generally because a man is not giving her his full attention. He is hearing her with only part of his mind when she wants his full attention. To say, "You're not listening" doesn't convey the correct message, which is, "You are not giving me your full attention."

To a man, there is a world of difference between these two statements. He can't argue with the second message, but the first only pushes him farther away.

When a man is half-listening, distracted, or looking away while she is talking, women quite commonly communicate the message that he is not listening by raising their voices. Getting louder for a woman is another way of saying, "You're not listening." The result, however, is the same; in the end he will listen less. Yelling at children also programs them to not listen.

Negative critical feedback just doesn't work. For most women, the only other option is to get upset and walk away. Although her options seem bleak, there is hope. By learning to pause and prepare a man, a woman can immediately begin getting the results she wants.

The Thirty-Second Attention Span

Many times, when a woman talks about her day, a man will focus on her for a moment, realize that she is going to talk for a while, and then pick up a magazine and begin reading it until she "gets to the point." If he is watching TV, he will listen for a few moments and then shift back to watching TV.

At the most, he will listen for about thirty seconds and then, when he experiences that she is not talking in a linear fashion, he automatically finds another focus for his masculine side. The news is great for focusing, since in the first paragraph of each article he gets the bottom line of who, what, where, when, how, and why.

In my seminars, I commonly ask how many women have experienced a man picking up a magazine to read soon after she begins to talk. Almost all the hands go up. I do this so that the women in the room can see that it is not just *their* husband who "doesn't listen."

Martha was one of those women. Her husband didn't take the course, but by learning at the seminar how to prepare a man to listen, she experienced an immediate and dramatic change. She was able to break through the thirty-second attention span and began getting his full attention.

Martha and Robert had been married for nine years. Quite commonly, when she talked he would briefly focus on her and then continue watching TV. Her reaction was to keep talking and then after a while get furious with him and complain that he didn't listen to her. Although this approach is certainly instinctive on her part, it doesn't work.

For years this pattern repeated itself. Even though Martha complained, Robert would still watch TV while she talked. If the TV wasn't on, he would pick up a magazine and read it while she was talking. Like many thousands of women, Martha was definitely not getting the support she most needed.

Robert didn't give her his full attention because he didn't feel the same need to talk about his day with someone giving him their full attention. It is not that he wasn't interested in *her,* it was that he wasn't interested in the details of her day.

To him, the details were unimportant unless they were directly related to some point. Men are used to organizing details in a logical manner to make a point or to figure out a solution. When a woman talks just to relax and connect with her partner, she commonly uses details that are not necessarily related to any point or solution. She is talking to share an experience, not fix it. When he recognized that she wasn't going to get to a point, he would then look back to the TV or pick up a magazine to find a point to focus on.

A man needs to have a goal or a focal point. At those times when a woman is sharing feelings, a man's mind begins to tense up while trying to find the point. When he realizes that it's going to be a while before she gets to her point, he relaxes his mind by focusing on a newspaper, magazine, or TV. He is generally not trying to be rude. Many times, he doesn't even know that he is doing it.

He Thinks He Is Listening

When a woman talks and a man looks away, he still believes he is listening. There is still a part of his mind following her words for when she gets to the point and his response is called for. In a sense, he is waiting for his turn to "do something." A small part of him is paying attention, scanning what she is saying for any problems that may require his full attention to solve. When she says he is not listening, it doesn't make sense to him because he knows that it's not completely true.

As long as she complains that he is not listening, he will never hear her actual message. What she is really saying is, "When you watch TV, I don't feel that I have your full attention. If you give it to me and turn off the TV, it will help me get this out much faster and it will feel very good." This is a message that a man can hear and understand. It also gives him a focus or reason to listen.

When a woman doesn't understand the way a man thinks and talks, she mistakenly assumes that he doesn't care about her. Martha was ready to end her marriage because she had become convinced that TV was more important to Robert than she was. When he picked up a magazine as she talked, she thought he hated her.

Quite commonly, they would argue about whether he was really listening or not.

She said, "You're not listening."

He said, "I am listening."

She said, "You can't listen and watch the TV at the same time."

He said, "How do you know what I can do?"

She said, "Well, I know I can't talk to you."

He said, "Look, I'm watching TV now, and I am hearing everything you are saying. I can repeat back everything you have said."

She said, "I knew it, I can't talk with you."

Various versions of this same argument went on for years until Martha tried a different approach.

The next time Robert picked up a magazine, instead of complaining or storming off in frustration Martha practiced a new skill. She paused from talking and looked *with* him at his magazine. After thirty seconds, he noticed that she had stopped talking. By pausing, she got his attention, and he remembered that she was talking.

Then she said, "Thanks, I really appreciate it when you give me your full attention. This will only take about three more minutes. Is that OK for you?"

After talking for about three minutes, she then thanked him for giving her his full attention. Instead of fighting about who was wrong, Martha got what she wanted. Robert started giving her his full attention when she spoke. Whenever he'd forget, she knew just what to do to get it back.

By gradually experiencing how much Martha appreciated and thrived on his full attention, Robert was instinctively motivated to give her his full attention when she talked.

When a woman wants a man to listen, it is important to make sure that he feels there will be closure. He needs to know what is required of him, how long it will take, and what he will get in return.

In this case, Martha let him know in positive and clear terms that she needed his full attention (not just for him to listen). She let him know it would only take three minutes, and when she was done, she let him know how much she appreciated it.

Three minutes is a good starting-out time for a man to practice building up his emotional support muscles. As he can do that, then she can begin to go on for longer and longer periods of time. Gradually, Martha would increase the time of her sharing.

When she noticed him starting to get frustrated, she would again pause and prepare him to listen by saying, "It will only be another three minutes and I'll be done." This kind of support for him ensured that he gradually learned how to support her. If she had more to say, then she used another new skill. She "postponed" sharing her feelings for another time.

A Woman's Lifeline

Good communication is a modern woman's lifeline. Without it, she loses touch with her ability to feel the love in her heart and receive the loving support of others; she loses her ability to feel warm, tender, and sweet feelings. By learning to support a man in a particular way, she can ensure getting back the support she needs to nurture her female side.

To achieve this end, it is important for her to realize that men have never been required to be good listeners of a woman's feelings and that they don't know how. By clearly understanding this fact, it gives her the patience and the awareness to appreciate each step he makes toward her fulfillment.

Women generally feel that if a man loves them, he will want to listen to their feelings. A man doesn't feel this way because sharing feelings is not as important to him and, traditionally, women didn't want to share their feelings with men.

It actually works the other way around. The more a man cares, if he hasn't learned how to duck and dodge it hurts more when he gets hit. When she is unhappy, it is much harder for him to listen without feeling blamed. It is harder because the more he loves her, the more he feels like a failure when she is not feeling loved and supported.

By understanding that a man really needs her support to support her successfully, a woman can then be motivated to help him without feeling as if she is begging for love. This insight that a man could deeply care but also resist her when she starts sharing feelings helps her to take responsibility for communicating in ways that are supportive for her and also for him.

The Importance of Timing

I've already mentioned how vital timing is to good communication. When a man is recuperating from the demands of his workday, it is counterproductive to make more demands on him. Until he becomes proficient in the art of listening, trying to converse when he first comes home feels to him like more work, which he will tend to resist. Even if he is eager, his mind will wander to something less demanding like the TV or a magazine. To fight this innate tendency is useless, but by working with it a woman can get what she needs.

I explored in great detail this tendency men have to temporarily pull away from a relationship to recharge and described it as cave time. I first heard this concept from a Native American woman who said that in her tribe, when a woman was married the mother gave her this wise warning: "When a man loves you, at times he will pull away and go to his cave. A woman should never try to follow him or else she will be burned by the dragon. After some time, he will be back and everything will be fine."

Cave time for a man is solitary time when he can most effectively recuperate from the day, forget his problems by staring off into the fire, and gradually connect with his loving feelings and remember what is most important to him. Once he feels better, he automatically comes out of the cave and is available for a relationship.

To ensure mutually supportive conversations, a woman needs to postpone her immediate needs to share her feelings until her male partner is out of the cave. It is disastrous to initiate a conversation before a man is actually capable of listening and sharing. Through "pausing" in this way and waiting for the right time to share her feelings, a woman can get the support she most needs.

One woman in my seminar shared that she was a cave buster. She would use dynamite to get in his cave, only to find that her husband would dig deeper and deeper tunnels. Without an understanding that her husband needed solitary time, trying to get closer only pushed him farther away.

When a man can't take the time he needs for himself, it is extremely difficult for him to find the loving feelings that originally attracted him to his partner. In a similar way, when a woman doesn't get the chance to share her feelings and connect with her female side, she, as well, loses touch with her deep, loving feelings.

Understanding the Cave

Most women do not understand the cave, nor do they recognize when a man is out. A woman is easily frustrated because she feels the need to talk but doesn't know how long it will take before he comes out. She wants him to come out, but she doesn't know what she can do to help. This uncertainty makes her need to talk even more urgent.

Men in relationships experience a similar frustration when women talk about problems. A man doesn't know how long she will talk before she feels better. He is afraid she will never be happy. It is hard for a man to figure out when she wants his advice or when she just wants to talk.

In a similar way, it is hard for a woman to understand if he is watching TV because there is nothing else to do or if he is in his cave and is not open to having a conversation. To solve these common problems, we not only need to understand our differences but must learn new skills for getting what we need.

The Need for Clear Signals

A woman needs clear communication signals to know when a man is open and when he is closed, in the same way that a man needs to know when she is open to solutions and when she just needs to be heard.

Just as it is hard for a man to trust that a woman will feel better again after sharing negative feelings, it is equally difficult for a woman to trust that a man loves her when he pulls away and ignores her.

To pause before talking or making requests of a man, a woman needs to first know if he is in the cave. If he is not available, she needs to postpone getting her needs met by him. If she can support him in this way, not only will he spend less time in the cave, he will be much more loving when he is out of the cave.

Through persisting in this process of not trying to change him but instead trying to assist him in being successful in supporting her, a woman can dramatically improve her relationship.

When a man is in his cave, it is the time for a woman to be less demanding of him. This nondemanding and trusting attitude is very attractive to a man, and will definitely shorten cave time.

When Is a Man out of His Cave?

Even when a woman begins to understand a man's need to be in the cave, it is still difficult to tell when he is out. Women persistently ask me, "How do I know when it is a good time to talk? How do I know when he is in the cave?"

My favorite example to answer this question has to do with my daughter Lauren. One evening when she was seven years old she had attended one of my lectures on the differences between men and women. Although much of the time she was playing in the back, she had actually taken in a lot.

In that lecture I talked about not going into a man's cave. I hadn't thought Lauren was listening, but on the way home she said, "Daddy, you said if you go into a man's cave you get burned by the dragon. Is that why sometimes you get angry at me? Is that just your dragon? Do you still love me?"

I said, "That's right. Sometimes I am in my cave and just need to be alone for a while and then I come out again. Even if sometimes I feel frustrated or angry with you, I still love you very much."

She said, "Thank you, Daddy, I'm sure glad I know about the cave."

The next day she came up to me while I was reading the newspaper and said, "Daddy, are you in your cave? I don't want to bother you if you are 'cause I don't want to be burned by the dragon." I told her that I was in the cave, but soon I would be out.

She then said, "Would you let me know when you are out, because I want to tell you about my day."

When I finished reading the paper, I then easily remembered to find my daughter and ask her about her day.

Sometimes the answer to the most complex problems can be right before our eyes. Volumes of books have been written trying to answer the question of how to get a man to open up and yet, given the right understanding, a little child could find the answer.

The way to tell if a man is in his cave is simply to ask. Although it sounds simple, it does take a lot of practice not to feel rejected if he doesn't want to talk. It is hard for a woman to ask because instinctively it is a shock to her when a man doesn't want to talk.

This is because when she loves a man and feels safe to share her feelings, then after a long day she looks forward to sharing and talking with him. When she wants to talk and he doesn't, it is embarrassing. It feels as though she loves him more than he loves her.

Signals That He Is out of the Cave

The way a man can help a woman know when he is out of the cave is to give her clear signals in a language that she will understand. Touching a woman in a nonsexual but affectionate way is probably the most effective and simple way.

When I am out of the cave and available for conversation, I search out my wife and touch her in some affectionate way or offer to give her a hug. This clear signal tells her that I am approachable.

This certainty regarding when I am available and when I am not makes a world of difference for her. She does not have to worry or try to figure out my moods.

When a man is out of the cave, it is even more helpful for her to recognize it if he initiates a conversation. This does not mean that he has to talk much. It means that he briefly communicates the message that he is out and is open to hearing her. This is best done by simply asking her a question about her day.

Initiating a conversation is particularly helpful because women today are many times so much in their male sides that they don't even know they need to talk until they are asked. Particularly if she has been burned in the past while sharing her feelings she will not consciously feel the need to talk.

Pausing to Postpone Sharing Feelings

A woman has to work hard at not reacting in a way that says to a man that he is a bad boy and that he is not making "Mommy" happy. To support him, she is required to nurture him with an accepting love and not be a mother trying to teach him how to be "good."

Even if these messages are her true feelings, when he is on his way to the cave it is not the time to share those feelings. To accomplish this feat she needs to practice "postponing" her feelings until she has a more receptive listener.

These kinds of feelings are a negative influence on him and are best shared with a woman friend. Through putting off giving a negative message she ensures that he will come back sooner. It is much easier for her to give him this support when she clearly knows when he is in the cave and that he will come out of his own accord.

If I am in a bad mood and needing cave time, quite commonly I will go for a drive. All I need to say is, "I need to go for a drive," and my wife understands that I am in my cave. My car is actually black with a black interior. To me, it feels like a moving cave. If I am watching TV and I am in my cave, I will scan the channels with my remote control at the commercial breaks. If I am open and receptive to her, then at the commercials I put the TV on mute and talk with her.

Generally speaking, when a man does something that a woman thinks is a waste of time or is unproductive, he is in his cave. It could be fiddling with his computer or fiddling with an old car in the garage. For some men, their cave is the workshop in the garage, a walk over the hill, a jog around the neighborhood, a workout at the gym, or going to a movie.

How to Ask a Man to Talk

Unless a man understands the importance of making clear signals that he is in the cave, a woman must depend on herself to figure it out. Even if a man knows the importance of giving signals, he will inevitably forget at times to use them. This being the case, it is essential for women to be skilled in checking out when he is in the cave and when he is not.

When a woman wants to talk, instead of assuming that a man is immediately available she needs to first "pause" and then approach him to see if it is the right time for him. She can "check it out" in a variety of ways.

By asking a man questions about his day she can quickly tell if he is in the mood to talk. If she asks, "How was your day?" and he gives a short answer like, "OK" or "Fine," it's a clear signal that he is in his cave or that he is open to having a conversation but would prefer that she talk more.

She can then say, "Is this a good time to talk, or would you like to do it later?"

If he is not deep in his cave, he will generally say, "This is a good time." Although he may still feel some resistance, it is not because he is in his cave or because he doesn't care, but because he doesn't have much to say. Don't be disappointed if he doesn't say, "Oh, thanks for asking, I would love to talk."

If he is hesitant but clearly says, "Not right now," then she can say, "OK, I'll check back later. How about twenty minutes?"

Generally speaking, that should be enough time. If he needs more time, it is important to be prepared to accept what he needs. The more gracious and nondemanding she is, the more he will think about taking the time to talk.

This situation is similar to when a man reaches out and gently touches his wife; he cannot expect that she should always receive his touch with a warm, loving response. If she pulls back and he doesn't react with anger but dodges and remains open to her, then she is much more willing to open up to him.

In a like manner, the more space or acceptance a woman can give a man while letting him know that she is looking forward to talking, the more open and willing he will be to make the time to talk.

The Unspoken Rules for Communicating

If a woman wants to talk with someone, she generally waits for her turn. It is her way of being polite. She either listens for a while and then begins to talk, or waits until the other person asks her about her day.

These unspoken rules are foreign to most men. If a woman waits for her mate to talk first, she may never get the chance to talk because he doesn't automatically have a lot to say.

A man's unspoken rules are that if you have something to say, say it. He doesn't feel the need to wait to be asked. If he wants to talk, he talks. When he asks questions, he rarely has the expectation that she is supposed to ask questions back.

When a woman asks him questions and he does talk, he thinks he is pleasing her by answering her questions.

Even if a man has learned that a woman wants him to ask her questions about her day, he will tend to forget. When she is asking him questions, he is so busy thinking of what to say that it is hard for him to remember to ask her about her day.

If a man gives short answers, a woman does not need to wait until he has had his turn. He doesn't mind if she begins talking about her day. It would not be rude to him if she began talking about her own day without first listening to him.

Men Who Talk Too Much

A single woman at one of my relationship seminars asked this question. She said, "You say men don't want to talk. My experience is with men who talk too much and don't listen to what I have to say. How do I get them to listen?"

I asked her if she herself was a good listener. She very proudly said yes. I then asked if *she* asked lots of questions. She again proudly said yes.

She then said, "I do all the right things, but they still don't listen to me."

I said, "You are doing all the right things to get a woman to listen, but not a man. If you want a man to stop talking and listen more, then you have to stop asking him questions."

The more a man has to think about answering questions, the less he will think about her or pause to let her talk.

To get a man's full attention, this woman first needed to stop asking more questions. Then, when he paused, she should say something like this: "That makes sense to me because . . ."

With this kind of lead-in phrase, a woman can get any man's attention. Men love to be acknowledged for making sense. These three simple words, "That makes sense," are so soothing to a man that he will immediately stop talking and listen to what she has to say.

The most effective way to get a man's full attention is to "prepare" him for the conversation by letting him off the hook of needing to talk more. By letting him know in advance that he doesn't have to talk, he can relax and listen instead of figuring out what to say. After all, she is the one who wants to talk.

This is a very important awareness. A man can be out of the cave and be open to conversation but not have anything to say. Instinctively, he doesn't feel the need to initiate conversation. When a woman senses that he doesn't have anything to say, she feels awkward talking more or asking him to listen as I have suggested.

It feels rude to her to say something like, "Well, even if you don't feel like talking, I have a lot to say. Would you listen to me? You don't have to say anything." She doesn't know that to him this is not rudeness. It is directness, and it is not demanding. Men love this kind of support.

By being prepared in this way, a man doesn't need to resist the listening process because it is clearly stated that he doesn't have to say anything.

Why Women Don't Initiate Conversations

There are actually many times when a man is out of the cave and available to have a conversation but is waiting for a woman to initiate the conversation. She may not know this because at other times when he was in the cave, she tried conversations only to find that getting him to talk was like pulling teeth.

After a few futile stabs at conversations, many women give up without even knowing it. They actually believe that they have nothing to say and don't want to talk. When they get home, they go into their caves as well.

These women do not realize they are missing out on the thing that can bring them the greatest happiness. Life has taught them that it is foolish to try and share feelings with a man. But with new relationship skills and a new job description, they can get the support and respect that they require in order to risk sharing their feminine feelings.

Still other women know that they are missing out, but blame the men for not wanting to talk. Their mothers did not teach them about the cave. The worst thing a woman can do is to blame a man for not wanting to talk. It would be like a man blaming a woman for talking too much. Neither approach is valid or productive.

New Communication Skills

To ensure the best communication in a relationship, both men and women can begin applying new skills. An easy way for women to remember what is required of them is to remember the four P's: pausing, preparing, postponing, and persisting. In a similar way, men can remember the four D's: ducking, dodging, disarming, and delivering. A relationship will be easiest when both are doing their best. Without these insights, relationships are much more difficult than they need to be.

Even when a woman's husband or boyfriend has not read this book, by applying these skills she will begin to get so much more. She will learn to talk in ways that are natural for her but that will also motivate him to listen and support more. This summary of the four P's can be helpful for a woman to remember what the basics are for getting the support she needs.

1. Pause
   A. Check it out. Ask him if this is a good time.
   B. Don't interrupt him if you know he is in the cave.

2. Prepare
   A. Set a time limit. Tell him how long it will take. When a man doesn't know where the conversation is going, he begins to panic. When he knows there is a time limit, then he can relax.
   B. Give him a clear job description. Tell him that he doesn't have to say anything or make other supportive comments.
   C. Encourage him. Occasionally remind him that he is not being blamed or that you understand it is hard to listen.
   D. Appreciate him. Each time when you are finished talking, let him know that you really appreciate his listening and that you feel much better because of his support.

3. Postpone
   A. When he is in his cave, postpone sharing your needs for another time when he is more available and able to give.
   B. Put off expecting him to do more until he has become proficient in listening more to feelings, then begin to ask for more physical help in small increments.
   C. When you are feeling blame or criticism, talk to someone else first to become more loving and centered and then talk to your partner.

4. Persist
   A. Continue giving him the support he needs to support you. Don't expect him to always remember.

B. When he resists conversation, persist in asking him to listen even if he has little or nothing to say.

C. Overcome the tendency to give in and not communicate with him. Patiently persist in practicing these skills.

One of the biggest obstacles to practicing the four skills for women and the four skills for men is not understanding that men and women essentially speak different languages. A man could be growing in his skills slowly but surely, but when he fails to listen or respect her feelings, she feels it is hopeless. In a similar way, a woman will be progressing in supporting her male partner, and then when she forgets to pause and prepare and he feels blamed, he may automatically assume that nothing is working.

Through understanding the different languages we speak it is much easier to recognize that our partners do love us and that they, in their own way, are doing their best.

4

Keeping the Magic of Love Alive

One of the paradoxes of loving relationships is that when things are going well and we are feeling loved, we may suddenly find ourselves emotionally distancing our partners or reacting to them in unloving ways. Maybe you can relate to some of these examples:

1. You may be feeling a lot of love for your partner, and then, the next morning, you wake up and are annoyed and resentful of him or her.

2. You are loving, patient, and accepting, and then, the next day, you become demanding or dissatisfied.

3. You can't imagine not loving your partner, and then, the next day, you have an argument and suddenly begin thinking about divorce.

4. Your partner does something loving for you, and you feel resentful for the times in the past when he or she ignored you.

5. You are attracted to your partner, and then suddenly you feel numb in his or her presence.

6. You are happy with your partner and then suddenly feel insecure about the relationship or powerless to get what you need.

7. You feel confident and assured that your partner loves you and suddenly you feel desperate and needy.

8. You are generous with your love, and then suddenly you become withholding, judgmental, critical, angry, or controlling.

9. You are attracted to your partner, and then when he or she makes a commitment you lose your attraction or you find others more attractive.

10. You want to be physically intimate with your partner, but when he or she wants it, you don't want it.

11. You feel good about yourself and your life and then, suddenly, you begin feeling unworthy, abandoned, and inadequate.

12. You have a wonderful day and look forward to seeing your partner, but when you see him or her, something that your partner says makes you feel disappointed, depressed, repelled, tired, or emotionally distant.

Maybe you have noticed your partner going through some of these changes as well. Take a moment to reread the above list, thinking about how your partner may suddenly lose his or her ability to give you the love you deserve. Probably you have experienced his or her sudden shifts at times. It is very common for two people who are madly in love one day to hate each other or fight the very next day.

These sudden shifts are confusing. Yet they are common. If we don't understand why they happen we may think we are going crazy, or we may mistakenly conclude that our love has died. Fortunately there is an explanation.

Love brings up our unresolved feelings. One day we are feeling loved, and the next day we are suddenly afraid to trust love. The painful memories of being rejected begin to surface when we are faced with trusting and accepting our partner's love.

Whenever we are loving ourselves more or being loved by others, repressed feelings tend to come up and temporarily overshadow our loving awareness. They come up to be healed and released. We may suddenly become irritable, defensive, critical, resentful, demanding, numb, or angry.

Feelings that we could not express in our past suddenly flood our consciousness when we are safe to feel. Love thaws out our repressed feelings, and gradually these unresolved feelings begin to surface into our relationship.

It is as though your unresolved feelings wait until you are feeling loved, and then they come up to be healed. We are all walking around with a bundle of unresolved feelings, the wounds from our past, that lie dormant within us until the time comes when we feel loved. Then, when we feel safe to be ourselves, our hurt feelings come up.

If we can successfully deal with those feelings, then we feel much better and enliven more of our creative, loving potential. If, however, we get into a fight and blame our partner instead of healing our past, we just get upset and then suppress the feelings again.

How Repressed Feelings Come Up

The problem is that repressed feelings don't come up saying, "Hi, I am your unresolved feelings from the past." If your feelings of abandonment or rejection from childhood start coming up, then you will feel you are being abandoned or rejected by your partner. The pain of the past is projected onto the present. Things that normally would not be a big deal hurt a lot.

For years we have suppressed our painful feelings. Then one day we fall in love, and love makes us feel safe enough to open up and become aware of our feelings. Love opens us up and we start to feel our pain.

Why Couples May Fight During Good Times

Our past feelings suddenly come up not just when we fall in love but at other times when we are feeling really good, happy, or loving. At these positive times, couples may unexplainably fight when it seems as though they should be happy.

For example, couples may fight when they move into a new home, redecorate, attend a graduation, a religious celebration, or a wedding, receive presents, go on a vacation or car ride, finish a project, celebrate Christmas or Thanksgiving, decide to change a negative habit, buy a new car, make a positive career change, win a lottery, make a lot of money, decide to spend a lot of money, or have great love making.

At all of these special occasions one or both partners may suddenly experience unexplained moods and reactions; the upset tends to be either before, during, or right after the occasion. It may be very insight-ful to review the above list of special occasions and reflect on how your parents might have experienced these occasions as well as reflect on how you have experienced these occasions in your relationships.

The 90/10 Principle

By understanding how past unresolved feelings periodically surface, it is easy to understand why we can become so easily hurt by our partners. When we are upset, about 90 percent of the upset is related to our past and has nothing to do with what we think is upsetting us. Generally only about 10 percent of our upset is appropriate to the present experience.

Let's look at an example. If our partner seems a little critical of us, it may hurt our feelings a little. But because we are adults we are capable of understanding that they don't mean to be critical or maybe we see that they had a bad day. This understanding prevents their criticism from being too hurtful. We don't take it personally.

But on another day their criticism is very painful. On this other day our wounded feelings from the past are on their way up. As a result we are more vulnerable to our partner's criticism. It hurts a lot because as a child we were criticized severely. Our partner's criticism hurts more because it triggers our past hurt as well.

As a child we were not able to understand that we were innocent and that our parents' negativity was their problem. In childhood we take all criticism, rejection, and blame personally.

When these unresolved feelings from childhood are coming up, we easily interpret our partner's comments as criticism, rejection, and blame. Having adult discussions at these times is hard. Everything is misunderstood. When our partner seems critical, 10 percent of our reaction relates to their effect on us and 90 percent relates to our past.

Imagine someone poking your arm a little or gently bumping into you. It doesn't hurt a lot. Now imagine you have an open wound or sore and someone starts poking at it or bumps into you. It hurts much more. In the same way, if unresolved feelings are coming up, we will be overly sensitive to the normal pokes and bumps of relating.

In the beginning of a relationship we may not be as sensitive. It takes time for our past feelings to come up. But when they do come up, we react differently to our partners. In most relationships, 90 percent of what is upsetting to us would not be upsetting if our past unresolved feelings were not coming up.

How We Can Support Each Other

When a man's past comes up, he generally heads for his cave. He is overly sensitive at those times and needs a lot of acceptance. When a woman's past comes up is when her self-esteem crashes. She descends into the well of her feelings and needs tender loving care.

This insight helps you to control your feelings when they come up. If you are upset with your partner, before confronting him or her first write out your feelings on paper. Through the process of writing Love Letters your negativity will be automatically released and your past hurt will be healed. Love Letters help center you in present time so that you can respond to your partner in a more trusting, accepting, understanding, and forgiving way.

Understanding the 90/10 principle also helps when your partner is reacting strongly to you. Knowing that he or she is being influenced by the past can help you to be more understanding and supportive.

Never tell your partner, when it appears as though their "stuff" is coming up, that they are overreacting. That just hurts them more. If you poked someone right in the middle of a wound you wouldn't tell them they were overreacting.

Understanding how the feelings of the past come up gives us a greater understanding of why our partners react the way they do. It is part of their healing process. Give them some time to cool off and become centered again. If it is too difficult to listen to their feelings, encourage them to write you a Love Letter before you talk about what was so upsetting.

A Healing Letter

Understanding how your past affects your present reactions helps you heal your feelings. If your partner has upset you in some way, write them a Love Letter, and while you are writing ask yourself how this relates to your past. As you write you may find memories coming up from your past and discover that you are really upset with your own mother or father. At this point continue writing but now address your letter to your parent. Then write a loving Response Letter. Share this letter with your partner.

They will like hearing your letter. It feels great when your partner takes responsibility for the 90 percent of their hurt that comes from the past. Without this understanding of our past we tend to blame our partners, or at least they feel blamed.

If you want your partner to be more sensitive to your feelings, let them experience the painful feelings of your past. Then they can understand your sensitivities. Love Letters are an excellent opportunity to do this.

You Are Never Upset for the Reason You Think

As you practice writing Love Letters and exploring your feelings you will begin to discover that generally you are upset for different reasons than you first think. By experiencing and feeling the deeper reasons, negativity tends to disappear. Just as we suddenly can be gripped by negative emotions we can also suddenly release them. These are a few examples:

1. One morning Jim woke up feeling annoyed with his partner. Whatever she did disturbed him. As he wrote her a Love Letter he discovered that he was really upset with his mother for being so controlling. These feelings were just coming up, so he wrote a short Love Letter to his mother. To write this letter he imagined he was back when he was feeling controlled. After he wrote the letter suddenly he was no longer upset with his partner.

2. After months of falling in love, Lisa suddenly became critical of her partner. As she wrote a Love Letter she discovered that she was really feeling afraid that she was not good enough for him and afraid he was no longer interested in her. By becoming aware of her deeper fears she started to feel her loving feelings again.

3. After spending a romantic evening together, Bill and Jean got in a terrible fight the next day. It started when Jean became a little angry with him for forgetting to do something. Instead of being his usual understanding self, suddenly Bill felt like he

wanted a divorce. Later as he wrote a Love Letter he realized he was really afraid of being left or abandoned. He remembered how he felt as a child when his parents fought. He wrote a letter to his parents, and suddenly he felt loving toward his wife again.

4. Susan's husband, Tom, was busy meeting a deadline at work. When he came home Susan felt extremely resentful and angry. One part of her understood the stress he was under, but emotionally she was still angry. While writing him a Love Letter she discovered that she was angry with her father for leaving her alone with her abusive mother. As a child she had felt powerless and abandoned, and these feelings were again coming up to be healed. She wrote a Love Letter to her father and suddenly she was no longer angry with Tom.

5. Rachel was attracted to Phil until he said he loved her and wanted to make a commitment. The next day her mood suddenly changed. She began to have a lot of doubts and her passion disappeared. As she wrote him a Love Letter she discovered that she was angry with her father for being so passive and hurting her mother. After she wrote a Love Letter to her father and released her negative feelings, she suddenly felt attracted again to Phil.

As you begin practicing Love Letters, you may not always experience past memories and feelings. But as you open up and go deeper into your feelings, it will become clearer that when you are really upset it is about something in your past as well.

As you grow more intimate in your relationships, love increases. As a result, deeper, more painful feelings will come up that need to be healed—deep feelings like shame and fear. Because we generally do not know how to deal with these painful feelings, we become stuck.

To heal them we need to share them, but we are too afraid or ashamed to reveal what we are feeling. At such times we may become depressed, anxious, bored, resentful, or simply exhausted for no apparent reason at all. These are all symptoms of our "stuff" coming up and being blocked.

Instinctively you will want to either run away from love or increase your addictions. This is the time to work on your feelings and not run away. When deep feelings come up you would be very wise to get the help of a therapist.

When deep feelings come up, we project our feelings onto our partner. If we did not feel safe to express our feelings to our parents or a past partner, all of a sudden we cannot get in touch with our feelings in the presence of our *present* partner. At this point, no matter how supportive your partner is, when you are with your partner you will not feel safe. Feelings will be blocked.

It is a paradox: Because you feel safe with your partner, your deepest fears have a chance to surface. When they surface you become afraid and are unable to share what you feel. Your fear may even make you numb. When this happens the feelings that are coming up get stuck.

This is when having a counselor or therapist is tremendously helpful. When you are with someone you are not projecting your fears on, you can process the feelings that are coming up. But if you are only with your partner, you may feel numb.

This is why people with even very loving relationships may inevitably need the help of a therapist. Sharing in support groups also has this liberating effect. Being with others whom we don't know intimately but who are supportive creates an opening for our wounded feelings to be shared.

When our unresolved feelings are being projected on our intimate partner, he or she is powerless to help us. All our partner can do is encourage us to get support. Understanding how our past continues to affect our relationships frees us to accept the ebb and flow of love. We begin to trust love and its healing process. To keep the magic of love alive we must be flexible and adapt to the ongoing changing seasons of love.

The Seasons of Love

A relationship is like a garden. If it is to thrive it must be watered regularly. Special care must be given, taking into account the seasons as well as any unpredictable weather. New seeds must be sown and weeds must be pulled. Similarly, to keep the magic of love alive we must understand its seasons and nurture love's special needs.

The Springtime of Love

Falling in love is like springtime. We feel as though we will be happy forever. We cannot imagine not loving our partner. It is a time of innocence. Love seems eternal. It is a magical time when everything seems perfect and works effortlessly. Our partner seems to be the perfect fit. We effortlessly dance together in harmony and rejoice in our good fortune.

The Summer of Love

Throughout the summer of our love we realize our partner is not as perfect as we thought, and we have to work on our relationship. Not only is our partner from another planet, but he or she is also a human who makes mistakes and is flawed in certain ways.

Frustration and disappointment arise; weeds need to be uprooted and plants need extra watering under the hot sun. It is no longer easy to give love and get the love we need. We discover that we are not always happy, and we do not always feel loving. It is not our picture of love.

Many couples at this point become disillusioned. They do not want to work on a relationship. They unrealistically expect it to be spring all the time. They blame their partners and give up. They do not realize that love is not always easy; sometimes it requires hard work under a hot sun. In the summer season of love, we need to nurture our partner's needs as well as ask for and get the love we need. It doesn't happen automatically.

The Autumn of Love

As a result of tending the garden during the summer, we get to harvest the results of our hard work. Fall has come. It is a golden time—rich and fulfilling. We experience a more mature love that accepts and understands our partner's imperfections as well as our own. It is a time of thanksgiving and sharing. Having worked hard during summer we can relax and enjoy the love we have created.

The Winter of Love

Then the weather changes again, and winter comes. During the cold, barren months of winter, all of nature pulls back within itself. It is a time of rest, reflection, and renewal. This is a time in relationships when we experience our own unresolved pain or our shadow self. It is when our lid comes off and our painful feelings emerge. It is a time of solitary growth when we need to look more to ourselves than to our partners for love and fulfillment. It is a time of healing. This is the time when men hibernate in their caves and women sink to the bottom of their wells.

After loving and healing ourselves through the dark winter of love, then spring inevitably returns. Once again we are blessed with the feelings of hope, love, and an abundance of possibilities. Based on the inner healing and soul searching of our wintery journey, we are then able to open our hearts and feel the springtime of love.

Successful Relationships

After studying this guide for improving communication and getting what you want in your relationships, you are well prepared for having successful relationships. You have good reason to feel hopeful for yourself. You will weather well through the seasons of love.

I have witnessed thousands of couples transform their relationships—some literally overnight. They come on Saturday of my weekend relationship seminar and by dinnertime on Sunday they are in love again. By applying the insights you have gained through reading this book and by remembering that men are from Mars and women are from Venus you will experience the same success.

But I caution you to remember that love is seasonal. In spring it is easy, but in summer it is hard work. In autumn you may feel very generous and fulfilled, but in winter you will feel empty. The information you need to get through summer and work on your relationship is easily forgotten. The love you feel in fall is easily lost in winter.

In the summer of love, when things get difficult and you are not getting the love you need, quite suddenly you may forget everything you have learned in this book. In an instant it is all gone. You may begin to blame your partner and forget how to nurture their needs.

When the emptiness of winter sets in, you may feel hopeless. You may blame yourself and forget how to love and nurture yourself. You may doubt yourself and your partner. You may become cynical and feel like giving up. This is all a part of the cycle. It is always darkest before the dawn.

To be successful in our relationships we must accept and understand the different seasons of love. Sometimes love flows easily and automatically; at other times it requires effort. Sometimes our hearts are full and at other times we are empty. We must not expect our partners to always be loving or even to remember how to be loving. We must also give ourselves this gift of understanding and not expect to remember everything we have learned about being loving.

The process of learning requires not only hearing and applying but also forgetting and then remembering again. Throughout this book you have learned things that your parents could not teach you. They did not know. But now that you know, please be realistic. Give yourself permission to keep making mistakes. Many of the new insights you have gained will be forgotten for a time.

Education theory states that to learn something new we need to hear it two hundred times. We cannot expect ourselves (or our partners) to remember all of the new insights in this book. We must be patient and appreciative of their every little step. It takes time to work with these ideas and integrate them into your life.

Not only do we need to hear it two hundred times but we also need to unlearn what we have learned in the past. We are not innocent children learning how to have successful relationships. We have been programmed by our parents, by the culture we have grown up in, and by our own painful past experiences. Integrating this new wisdom of having loving relationships is a new challenge. You are a pioneer. You are traveling in new territory. Expect to be lost sometimes. Expect your partner to be lost. Use this guide as a map to lead you through uncharted lands again and again.

5

A Lifetime of Love and Passion

The high rate of divorce is not a sign that people today are less interested in marriage. On the contrary, it indicates that we want more from our relationships than ever before. Men and women alike are dissatisfied because their marital expectations are much greater than in the past. We want a lifetime of love; we want lasting passion with one special person.

Even with the high level of divorce, there is also a high rate of remarriage. If the flame of passion goes out, both men and women would rather risk the pain of divorce than the loss of feelings. We intuitively know that through continuing to nurture a special relationship something much greater can be experienced. Deep inside, we sense that passionate monogamy is possible, but we do not have the skills to fully experience it.

The enormous market for women's romance novels and TV soap operas is not the cause of this dissatisfaction but is actually the symptom of an unfulfilled desire for passion in our relationships.

These strong tendencies are not necessarily symptoms of dysfunction but are the natural expressions of a frustrated deeper need for emotional support in their relationships.

A Relationship Is an Investment

A relationship is like an investment. We give to our partner and hope over time to get more and more in return. Initially, getting the emotional support we are looking for may be difficult, but through the years, it becomes easier and easier.

Whether the partner finds out or not, the effect is there. On an intuitive level, the other partner loses the feeling that they are special. Without this feeling, love and passion cannot grow. It will then take years to recapture that "special" feeling.

Sometimes it takes the threat of permanent loss to make people appreciate what they have; sometimes the imminent death of a relationship must stare us in the face before we can feel our deep love and longing to live together. Just as a near-death experience will often motivate or inspire a person to greater heights, so also can an affair exert an inspirational influence on the relationship.

This does not imply that we should risk making our mates feel betrayed and rejected in order to bring feeling back into the relationship. There are other ways. Through practicing new relationship skills, we can revive the passion even if it has been declared dead.

The Seven Secrets of Lasting Passion

To sustain passion in a relationship, there are seven important secrets. To apply new skills in each of these areas, we will discuss each one in greater depth.

1. Differences Attract

The most important aspect of attraction is that we are different. Just as the positive and negative poles of a magnet always attract each other, when a man remains in touch with his masculinity and a woman feels her femininity, the attraction can be maintained in a relationship.

Having to give up who we are to please our partners ultimately kills the passion. By seeking to resolve our differences without having to deny our true selves, we ensure lasting attraction.

Without a doubt, a man feels most turned on and attracted to his partner when she makes him feel like a man. Likewise, a woman is most attracted to a man when he makes her feel totally feminine. By taking the time to make sure that we avoid emotional role reversal, we can maintain the attraction we feel to each other.

This attraction is not just physical. When passion is sustained, our curiosity and interest in our partners also grow over time. We find to our surprise that we are still interested in what our partners think, feel, and do.

Working with our differences is a requirement for keeping the passion alive. If we consistently have to give up or change who we are to please our partners, passion dies.

The most important differences that need to be nurtured are our gender differences. For a woman to stay attracted to a man, he must be in touch with and express his male side. It is fine for him to express his female side, but if he suppresses his male side to be in a relationship with her, she will eventually lose her attraction for him.

In a similar way, for a man to stay attracted to a woman she must continue to express her female side. She can also express the qualities of her male side, but if her female side is not available to him, he will turn off.

How a Woman Can Nurture Her Female Side

Besides using new relationship skills and assisting a man in supporting her, a woman—single or married—must take pains to nurture her female side. Here is a list of the many things she can do:

1. Taking more time each day to share in a nongoal-oriented way about the problems of her day. This is best done on a walk or by having lunch with someone she does not look to for solutions to her problems.

2. Getting a massage or some kind of nurturing body work every week is extremely valuable. Being physically touched in a nonsexual way is very important to relax her and bring her back to a pleasant awareness of her body.

3. Talking on the phone and/or staying in touch with friends and relatives. It is vitally important that she not let the pressures of work and keeping a family and home together prevent her from taking time to talk with friends.

4. Making regular time for prayer, meditation, yoga, exercise, writing in a journal, or working in the garden should be observed with great commitment. Ideally, she should create twenty to thirty minutes twice a day when she can just *be* without having to *do* anything for anyone.

5. Creating a working style that supports her feminine side. Practice enlisting the support of others rather than being too independent and autonomous. Never miss an opportunity to let a man carry a box for you or open the door. Have pictures of your family and friends around you while you work. When at all possible, surround yourself with beauty and flowers.

6. Getting at least four hugs a day from friends and family members.

7. Taking the time to write thank-you notes for the support you receive from others.

8. Varying routes home from work. Try to avoid the tendency to most efficiently get home each day by following the same route every time.

9. Becoming a tourist in your own town and regularly taking a mini vacation. Also try to get away from the home and enjoy new settings and vacations.

10. Joining a support group or visiting a therapist to make sure you can share your feelings freely without being concerned about your professional reputation.

11. Setting aside one evening a week for yourself. Go out and enjoy a movie or the theater, or stay home and take a

long, warm bath. Play beautiful music, light candles, and either read a wonderful book or turn down the lights and fantasize. Take the time to do what you would most enjoy doing.

12. Listing everything that needs to be done and then putting in big letters at the top, "Things that don't have to be done immediately." Take at least one day a month to rest and not solve *any* problems. If you are a mother, take the day off, and get away from your home and children.

To suddenly try to do everything on the above list would, in itself, be overwhelming. Post a customized version somewhere, and slowly but surely begin incorporating these suggestions. Without taking deliberate steps to nurture her female side, a woman today will tend to automatically stay in her masculine side and unknowingly sabotage not only her relationships but her relationship with herself as well.

Ways a Man Can Nurture His Masculine Side

In my seminars, men commonly ask how they can develop their masculine side—particularly if they are not in relationships and don't have a woman to appreciate their actions when they need support.

Whether a man is single or married, there are many things he can do to stay strong. He should pick and choose which suggestions are appropriate for him. Here is a list of twelve:

1. Spend time with other men competing on a team or individually. By channeling your competitive tendencies in a playful way, you are released from feeling so driven by your work. You are automatically released from measuring yourself only by your work. Watching your favorite sports on TV or going to a game has a similar cathartic effect.

2. Go to action movies. It is healthy for adult males to experience violence on the big screen, particularly if it is expressed skillfully and ultimately to protect others. Watching movies like *Rocky, The Terminator,* and *Universal Soldier* is a way for you to feel and redirect your own violent tendencies. When children, however, experience violence on TV or in the movies, it has the opposite effect: It creates more violence in them.

3. Take cave time in your relationships. You should not feel guilty saying no to others when you need to be alone to recharge. You should not feel obligated to talk when you don't feel like it. This does not mean that you should never talk but that you should carefully pick the times.

If you tend to rarely take cave time, then you should do it even though it is lonely and painful. In ancient times, a boy became a man by fasting alone for a week in the wilderness. His aloneness forced him away from his mother, or female side, and he found the man within.

In a similar way, a man doesn't continue to experience his male power unless he takes the risk to put himself in a situation where he needs his strength. Courage grows through doing courageous actions.

4. Make sure you exert your muscles every week. Lift weights, jog, ride a bike, climb a mountain, swim, et cetera. Make sure that at least once weekly you push your muscles to the point of strain or exhaustion. Press your limits.

5. Make sure your life doesn't get too comfortable and cushy. Do something each week that requires you to overcome your inner resistance to exerting your different strengths. That could mean getting up earlier than usual to finish a project or staying later to make sure that you did the best you could do. Apply discipline in order to build your male strength.

6. Try each week to do random acts of kindness—for others you care about or complete strangers. When an older person needs a seat, offer yours. While driving, when someone

needs to cut in, graciously slow down. Be magnanimous in your generosity.

When someone needs you and you feel like resting, make the effort to help them anyway. I am not saying that you should do this every time, but just occasionally.

7. When you are upset or angry, don't punish others. Instead, focus on your breathing. Count to five on the in breath and then count to five on the out breath. Count ten cycles of this process, and then start over until you are not upset.

8. Make a list of all the things you most enjoy doing. Make sure that you are creating time each week for your favorite hobby or hobbies. Do things that make you feel accomplished and in charge.

9. When something needs to be done that won't take a lot of time or energy, do it immediately. Repeatedly affirm inside, "Do it now!"

10. When you feel afraid to do something that would really be good to do, feel the fear and do it anyway. Take reasonable risks. It is better to have tried and failed than never to have tried.

11. Practice containing your anger. You can redirect it either through some physically constructive activity, or privately express your feelings in a journal. Look for other feelings underneath the anger. When you do express anger, ideally it should be without having to raise your voice, but in a firm, confident but centered, and nonintimidating manner.

12. Talk about feelings with male friends, or create a male support group. Don't rely primarily on women to heal or hear your feelings. It is very helpful for some men to experience gatherings of the "men's movement," reading poetry, telling and listening to the ancient myths, dancing, singing, or drumming.

Through these techniques, a man in a relationship can ensure that he doesn't swing too much to his female side. A single man can help strengthen his male side and attract a woman who will support his being both powerful and sensitive.

2. Change and Growth

Living with the same person can, over time, eventually become very boring if they are not regularly changing. Staying fresh is crucial for both partners in a marriage. Just as listening to a favorite song a hundred times in a row makes it grow stale, so also may our partners become boring if they do not grow and change.

Just as physical growth is so obvious in our children, we must always continue to grow emotionally, mentally, and spiritually. We must be careful not to sacrifice or deny ourselves too much. When a relationship does not allow us to grow, the passion between two people begins to fade.

Loving your partner does not mean spending all your time together. Too much time together can also make a relationship commonplace and devoid of mystery. Enjoying other friends and activities means that you can always bring back something new to the relationship. This applies to doing things separately from your partner and doing things with your partner and others. Having dinner with another couple on a regular basis is a good idea.

Good Communication

If a woman doesn't feel safe in talking about her feelings, she will eventually have nothing to say. Creating the safety for her to talk freely without her having to fear rejection, interruption, or ridicule allows a woman to thrive in a relationship. Over time, she can continue to trust and love her partner more if he is a good listener.

Men quite commonly grow bored when women tell them the details of their days. They are more interested in the bottom line. As a man begins to understand how to listen in an active way that his mate can appreciate, listening and sharing stops being a chore and becomes an important nurturing ritual. With open lines of communication, a woman will continue to grow.

Lots of Appreciation

When a man does not feel appreciated in a relationship, he also stops growing. He may not know why, but when he returns home he feels increasingly passive and disengaged from his partner. He stops initiating things to do. His routine becomes rigid and fixed.

What makes my relationship with my wife so uplifting is that she never expects me to do anything in the home. Almost every domestic responsibility I have doesn't feel like a chore that gets taken for granted, but is a gift that she appreciates as if I didn't have to do it. This makes me want to do it rather than feeling that I have to do it.

Creating Change

It is important to schedule special occasions. A man needs to remember that women tend to feel the weight of domestic responsibility and find it hard to take time off for themselves. If a man creates special times when she can get out of the routine, she is free to feel nurtured.

Celebrations, parties, presents, and cards also affirm the passage of time. They are particularly important for women. A woman greatly appreciates a man's special attention to her at these times. His remembering birthdays, anniversaries, Valentine's Day, and other holidays means a lot to a woman. Doing something special on those days for her frees her from feeling overwhelmed by life's repetitive responsibilities and assures her that she is loved.

One of the chief passion assassins is routine. Even if you are comfortable in your rut, it is helpful to break out of it from time to time. Even doing silly things can help make a moment special and memorable. For example, on our last vacation, instead of just taking a picture of my family in front of the Washington Monument, I lay down on the sidewalk and shot a picture from a lying-down position. Everyone laughed, and as a result, that moment will be remembered. All of our little efforts to occasionally break the routine make a difference.

Ultimately, what keeps passion alive in a relationship is growing in love. When, as a result of living, laughing, crying, and learning together two people are able to love and trust each other more, the passion will continue.

3. Feelings, Needs, and Vulnerabilities

To continue feeling our love, we need to feel. When it is not safe to have feelings or sensitivities, we quickly lose touch with our passion. While women need to talk more about their feelings and be heard if they are to feel vibrant in a relationship, men need to be appreciated for their actions if they are to feel like doing things for their partners.

When a man stops feeling a tender desire to please his partner, his tender feelings are automatically repressed. When a woman stops feeling the safety to share her feelings, she also begins to close up by repressing emotions.

Over time, when a woman or man continues to repress feelings, they begin to build walls around their hearts. Each time a woman feels ignored, minimized, and unsupported, another brick is placed in her wall. Each time a man attempts to be there for her and he ends up feeling ignored, criticized, corrected, or taken for granted, another brick is placed in his wall.

In the beginning, we can continue to feel love because the wall of repressed feelings is not fully blocking our hearts. But once it does, it cuts us off from our loving emotions.

To bring back the passion, this wall has to be dismantled brick by brick. Every time we remove one by applying advanced relationship skills, a little light begins to shine through. We then suddenly become aware of the rest of the wall and again feel that we are shut off. Slowly but surely, by continuing to successfully communicate and appreciate each other, that wall can come down and feelings can be fully experienced again.

Feeling Pain

When we are not getting the love we need, but remain vulnerable to our partners, we feel pain. Many couples deal with this by numbing themselves. They might say to themselves, "It doesn't matter, I don't care." They may begin to close up, saying, "I can't really trust him to be there for me, so I won't rely on him."

The most painful and lonely feeling is lying next to someone you don't feel you can reach out and touch with love. At this point, you may turn to an addiction to avoid feeling the pain of not being loved. Such dependencies free us from the pain but kill the passion. Only by learning to reach out for love and ask for what we want in skillful ways can we really heal our pain.

By turning off our feelings, we lose touch with our inner passion. We may not even know what we actually need more of because we have stopped feeling.

Working on Trust and Caring

The challenge women face in their relationships is to keep opening up when feeling disappointed or unloved. It is of paramount importance that they work on trusting their partners more and more and continue to be receptive. Otherwise, they will lose touch with their vulnerability and needs.

The secret to growing in trust is not to expect your partner to be perfect but to believe that you are growing in the skills that help you help him give you what you want. Through understanding how men are different, a woman enables herself to trust that he loves her even when he doesn't instinctively do the things *she* would do to demonstrate caring.

Over time, she can begin to see the ways in which he thinks he is loving her. Most important, she can apply advanced relationship skills to help him be more successful in supporting her.

To take down the wall around his heart, a man must work on caring. To bring back the passion, he needs to remember that it will require hard work and effort. At times, it will be like lifting a heavy weight.

If there is no wall around his heart, doing things is easy. Once he is taken for granted, the wall begins to rise again. Each time he feels his efforts are not appreciated, another brick is added to the wall.

But as he consciously begins doing little things that she can appreciate, if only for brief moments, the wall building stops. When his determination frays, and the wall suddenly looks higher, he becomes weary and resistant once more. He craves only to spend a lot of time in his cave.

A man can eventually come out and overcome the inertia of not caring if he is aware of the effort required to open his heart again. As he does, he will see that he is truly becoming a stronger person. With this strength, his road ahead will be less rocky. Eventually, he will be energized as never before by pleasing his partner.

Healthy Dependence

As we grow together in love and trust, open up and feel our mutual needs more strongly, our vulnerability increases too. Passion is most powerfully experienced when we know how much we need someone.

In the beginning of our marriage, securing Bonnie's appreciation was relatively unimportant to me. Over the years, I have grown to love receiving it.

After years of my consistently trying to be there for her, she can freely feel her needs for my love as well. The more she can depend on my support, the more passion she can feel. Bonnie is also realistic. She knows that I am not perfect and that I cannot always be there for her.

Bonnie's dependence on me is healthy because it is based on what I can really give her. This allows her to be more vulnerable, which in turn allows me to feel like I make a difference.

It is unwise as well as naive to expect our partners to always give us the love we need. Sometimes they have none to share and yet we demand more (in a sense, it is as though we are saying to a person in a wheelchair, "If you love me, then you will stand up and walk"). Sometimes they just can't be there for us in the ways we mistakenly think they can or should. But once we begin to need our partners in ways that they can't or don't support us, we will not only turn them off but will disappoint ourselves as well. When we need our partners too much, we will eventually pull away our trust and caring.

The more successful we are in fulfilling each other, the more we can rely on that support. With this kind of trust, even when our partners let us down, we will know that they did the best they could and we can be much more forgiving.

4. Personal Responsibility and Self-Healing

As we continue to open up and have our emotional needs met in a relationship, our unresolved past feelings ultimately begin to surface. When they rise up, they don't say, "Hi, I'm your anger with your dad." Instead, they are directed at our partners.

It is an irony that when we feel most loved, the unresolved feelings from past experiences of not being loved begin to affect our moods. One minute we are feeling passion, the next we are considering divorce. Such radical shifts we always justify by our partners' behavior, although it really isn't primarily about them.

For example, I come home in a great mood and my wife

greets me at the door by saying, "You forgot to call and tell me you were late. I didn't know what had happened." Certainly, I don't like being greeted with such a negative mothering statement, but if I suddenly get really upset and go to my cave and even consider divorce over that one statement, I have to take responsibility for my strong reaction.

Blaming your partner is looking in the wrong direction and aggravates the wound.

When past feelings begin to surface, they generally make us feel uncharacteristically negative. We may feel a lot of blame, criticism, doubt, resentment, confusion, ambivalence, judgment, and rejection. For a moment, we regress back to feeling and reacting the way we did as children when we didn't feel safe to freely react. When such feelings surface, it is vital for us to work on taking responsibility for being more loving and forgiving.

We should not expect our partners to be our loving parents. That, as we know, is a surefire passion killer. At those times, we need to parent ourselves, or work with a surrogate parent in a psychotherapeutic setting. It is up to us to re-parent ourselves, not our partners.

When we start blaming our partners for our unhappiness, it is a clear signal that our own "old stuff" is coming up. Although we feel especially entitled to demand more from our mates, we should demand nothing. It is a time for self-healing. It is a time for us to give ourselves the comfort and understanding that our parents may have failed to give us.

Remember, to expect our partners to make us feel better is to put them in the role of parents. The more dependent we become on them to change before *we* can change, the more stuck we will be. By parenting ourselves, we are free to release them from being the targets of our blame.

Feeling Powerless

Another signal that we are dealing with the past is powerlessness. Whenever we feel out of control and therefore seek to control another, our childhood is generally affecting us.

We *were* controlled as children. We were genuinely powerless to get what we wanted and needed. As adults we have many more choices and opportunities.

Even with new relationship skills you will at times feel like nothing is working and that you'll never get what you want. When this feeling emerges, we need to embrace it and sympathize with ourselves, but must also keep in mind that we are not really powerless. It is rather that our present assessment of the situation is definitely being clouded by old feelings seeking release. By applying self-healing techniques, a clearer vision of your abilities and opportunities will begin to come back into focus within minutes.

Impatience

When our hearts are open, we are patient toward our partners' limitations and our own. When strong feelings of impatience appear, they are another signal that childhood feelings are clouding our vision.

As adults we have learned how to wait patiently for desire to become reality. Patience is a skill and a part of maturity. When we suddenly begin to feel impatient, we lose our realistic perspective and immediately demand more than is possible.

Instead of feeling good that progress is being achieved, we feel frustrated that not enough is happening fast enough. With each setback, we negate our progress.

Quite commonly, after taking my seminar or reading my books, men will begin to make changes. Then, after a while, they stop. At that point, a woman may begin to feel, "I knew it, he didn't care. He's just going back to the way he always was." Her negativity prevents her from assisting him to continue supporting her.

If he offers to do something, she withers him with, "Well, I'll wait to see if you really do it before I get excited." There is no better way for him to lose his motivation.

When a woman becomes impatient, she will demand that her partner make his changes permanently instead of realizing that he is engaged in an ongoing process to give her the support she needs. Instead of giving up or demanding more, a woman needs to focus less on changing her partner and more on changing her own attitude.

Opening Our Hearts

If we feel we are not getting the love we need and are blaming our partners, it is a clear sign that we need something our partners simply cannot presently give us. Taking responsibility for supporting ourselves when our hearts are closed frees us from dwelling on our partners as the problem and allows us to examine the situation on a much more fundamental level. We are able to nurture ourselves and then come back to the relationship with more to give, not more to demand.

Instead of drowning in negativity and reacting in unloving ways when our hearts are closed, we can use this "downtime" for self-healing. Instead of looking to our partners to change when we are blaming them, we should focus on changing ourselves. When we are feeling open and forgiving, we can refocus and look for ways in which to solve or correct the problem that originally upset us.

The Feeling Letter Technique

A method I use to help release my negative feelings is called the feeling letter technique. By taking a few minutes to do this technique I can free myself from the grip of negative feelings and then feel more forgiving and agreeable.

For over twelve years I have used different versions of this technique and it still works dramatically for me at those times when I am not feeling very loving. It is a very powerful tool for both men and women.

Writing a feeling letter not only strengthens a man's ability to contain his feelings but is also helpful when he is on his female side and needs to be heard. Instead of dumping his negative feelings on his partner, he can write them out and achieve his goal more effectively than he could by talking.

A man can use this technique particularly when he needs to share his feelings but knows that this is not the time. As we have discussed, when a man displays more feeling or emotional vulnerability than a woman, it may push her to her male side. Rather than risk that, he should enact the following three steps.

This exercise is equally useful for a woman if she needs to share her feelings when her partner is in his cave and can't hear her. If she is feeling in the mood to blame or change her partner, it is also a good idea for her to practice this technique and get more centered before he returns.

Step One

Begin by writing out whatever you would have liked to say to your partner. It is perfectly OK to blame or sound critical.

Set down what makes you angry, sad, afraid, and sorry. Take a couple of minutes to dwell on each of these emotions. Even if you don't actually feel some of them, ask yourself what you would be experiencing if you did. For example, if you are not angry, write: "If I was the angry type, I would say . . ." Spend about two minutes on each of the emotions.

After taking a total of eight minutes to express your different emotions, take two more minutes to focus on writing out your wants, wishes, needs, or hopes, and then sign your name. In just ten minutes, you're done. Try not to spend more time than this unless, of course, you enjoy it and find an immediate release by writing out your feelings. With practice, this will automatically begin to happen.

Step Two

In step two, write a letter from your partner to you saying the things that you would want to hear him or her say. Pretend that you have shared your letter with your partner and that they have really heard you. Write out the words that would make you feel heard.

Have them first thank you for sharing your feelings. Then have them express an understanding of your feelings. Finally, have them apologize for their mistakes and make promises to support you better in the future. Even if your partner would not respond in such a positive way, use your imagination.

Take about three minutes to write this response letter. If it takes longer than that, it is certainly OK. Simply writing out the words you would want to hear will make you feel better. Even though your partner is not really saying these things, you will benefit by hearing them.

Step Three

In step three, take two minutes to respond back the way you probably would if your partner really did hear you and apologized for their mistakes. In this short forgiveness letter, be as specific as possible. Use the phrase "I forgive you for . . . ."

If it is still hard to forgive, remember that you are not saying that what they did is OK. When you forgive, you are clearly pointing out their mistakes but at the same time are releasing your tendency to continue withholding your love, compassion, and understanding.

Forgiveness doesn't mean the problem went away. It means that you are not closing yourself up to dealing with it in a loving manner. By practicing this feeling letter exercise at those times when you are resentful or your partner won't talk, you will suddenly feel relieved. Then you can patiently wait for the right opportunity to share your feelings, thoughts, and desires in a way that works for you, your partner, and the relationship.

5. Love, Romance, and Monogamy

Through taking responsibility for our reactions and actions in a relationship, we can truly begin to give and receive love successfully. Without an awareness of how our partners specifically need love, we may be missing priceless opportunities.

Women primarily feel loved when they are receiving from their men the emotional and physical support they need. It does not matter as much what he provides but that he does it in a continuous way. A women feels loved when she feels that a man's love is consistent.

When a man doesn't understand a woman, he tends to focus on the big ways to fulfill her all at once but will then ignore her for weeks. While good communication provides a healthy basis for a loving relationship, romance is the dessert. The way to a woman's heart is through doing lots of little things for her on a consistent basis.

What Romance Says

When a man does little things that say, "I care; I understand what you feel; I know what you like; I am happy to do things for you; and you are not alone," he is directly fulfilling a woman's need for romance. When a man does things without a woman having to ask, she feels deeply loved. If he forgets to do them, though, a wise woman graciously persists in reminding him by asking in a nondemanding manner.

A man, however, receives love differently from a woman. He chiefly feels loved when she lets him know again and again that he is doing a good job of fulfilling her. Her good mood makes him feel loved. Even when she enjoys the weather, a part of him takes the credit. A man is happiest when a woman is fulfilled.

While a woman feels romanced by the flowers, chocolates, greeting cards, et cetera, a man's sense of romance is fueled by a woman's appreciation of him. When he does little things for her and she appreciates it a lot, then he feels more romantic.

Women generally do not realize that the kind of love a man needs most is her loving message that he has fulfilled her.

When she is happy about the things he provides for her, he feels loved. When he can do something for her, he lets in her love. The most important skill for loving a man is to catch him when he is doing something right and notice and appreciate him for it. The most significant mistake is taking him for granted.

A man feels loved when he gets the message that he has made a difference, that he has been helpful in some way, and that his partner benefits from his presence. The other way to love a man is whenever possible to minimize his mistakes with statements like, "It's no big deal," or "It's OK." Downplaying disappointments makes him much more open to future requests and needs.

When a man does things for a woman and she is fulfilled, they both win. When I bring in the logs and build a fire, Bonnie feels special and cared for. Her romantic feelings begin to ignite. Knowing that, I am also quite pleased and confident.

However, when I sit on the couch and watch her bring in the logs and build a fire, although I feel relaxed and grateful, our romantic feelings aren't being charged. It is a very different dynamic that occurs when a woman takes care of a man.

Passionate Monogamy

Although women need romance to feel loved, for passion to grow over time their most important intimacy requirement is monogamy. A man can make the romantic gestures, but if he is not monogamous, her passion cannot grow. Romance tells a woman that she is special. And there is nothing that makes a woman feel more special than a man in touch with his passions and wanting only her.

As a woman ages, her ability to feel and express passion increases if she feels she can fully trust her partner to be there for her. If she feels she is being compared to another woman or that she has to compete, she cannot continue to open up.

If she senses that he is having an affair or could have an affair, she shuts down. Like a delicate rose she needs the clear and clean water of monogamy to gradually unfold, one petal at a time.

Not only does she benefit from monogamy but he does too! When a man is trusted by his wife and family, others sense something they can trust about him. Physical monogamy strengthens a man and makes him worthy of the highest trust.

In the famous bestseller, *Think and Grow Rich,* Napoleon Hill interviewed five hundred of the most successful men in America about the qualities that created success. Remarkably, all of the men were active in a passionate, monogamous relationship of over thirty years' duration.

These powerful, successful men had somehow learned to maintain passion with one woman for decades. Their fire had not burned out.

Greater drive and success are waiting for those men who realize this simple secret of love. Through creating and sustaining a passionate monogamous relationship, not only can a woman grow in passion but a man can be more powerful and effective in his work.

This study of only men was conducted many years ago. I am sure without a doubt that as women learn to master having careers in tandem with an ongoing passionate relationship, they too will be even more effective and influential in their work.

Knowing and sensing my ever-increasing physical fulfillment with her and my clear commitment to our monogamous relationship, Bonnie is more satisfied, more centered. Even though she is not with me when I am away, she continues to feel the special physical connection that only we share. I may share my mind and spirit with many, but only Bonnie gets my passionate energy.

Mental Monogamy

Not only are men not taught why monogamy is important, they are not taught how to be monogamous. The technique is very simple. When a man notices another woman and automatically starts getting turned on, he should just begin thinking about having sex with his wife, or he can just begin remembering a particularly exciting memory of passion with his wife. This way, each time he gets automatically turned on, his energy is consciously directed to his partner. After five to eight years of this practice, he will become even more attracted to his wife. He will also have learned to master his energy. Not only will his wife grow in passion with him, but he will have more power and success in his life.

6. Friendship, Autonomy, and Fun

Friendship is a breeze if we suppress our feelings. If one partner is willing to sacrifice who he or she is to the relationship, they will always get along—but the passion will die.

Make no mistake, although women quite commonly will "lose themselves" to accommodate their partners, men also surrender a major part of themselves. To avoid conflict, a man will also hold himself back. Without good communication skills, quite commonly a couple with a lot of love will choose to maintain the friendship and sacrifice their feelings. They do not realize that by suppressing negative feelings they are also suppressing their ability to feel in general.

When a woman cares for a man but doesn't help him in supporting her, she is actually hurting, not helping, the relationship. A man can only thrive in a relationship when he truly fulfills her needs. If she pretends to be fulfilled he will "think" he is fulfilled, but he doesn't even know what he is missing.

To be really good friends in a relationship requires a balance of autonomy and dependence. As we have explored, needing our partners is the basis of passion. However, if we are not also autonomous, at those times when our partners have little to give to us, we will feel powerless to get what we need.

Through practicing personal responsibility and self-healing we can nurture ourselves at those times when our partners can't be our nurturers. The real test of love is when we can be our partner's friend, and give without any expectation of return. This becomes easier when we are not too dependent on them and when at other times we have repeatedly experienced that they can be there for us. When we are confident that we can get what we need at other times, then we are not so demanding at those times when our partners have little to give.

Lightness and Fun

A man is almost always annoyed when a woman wants to "work on the relationship." He doesn't want to work on it. He would rather just live in it.

A man needs to feel that sometimes he is on vacation in the relationship and, in a sense, can do no wrong. He wants to feel that he is fine the way he is and that he is not required to change. When a woman says, "It's no big deal," or "It's OK," he tends to lighten up. When a woman can be lighthearted about her problems, a man feels like a success.

On the other hand, for a woman to feel friendship for a man it means that he can be relaxed about her getting upset. If he can just give her a little sympathy without taking the issue so personally, she can shift her feelings without making a scene.

Friendship for a woman means that her mate will, from time to time, go out of his way to support her or offer his help. Friendship for a man means that a woman will go out of her way not to be demanding or expect too much.

Being our partner's friend means never trying to change their mood or taking it personally when they are not feeling the way we want them to. Learning this lesson of detachment can totally transform a relationship.

Afterword

When *Men Are from Mars, Women Are from Venus* was first published in 1992, I told people that my vision for the book was that it would sell a million copies one day. Time has proven me wrong. As the last days of the twentieth century came to a close, the book had sold more than seven million copies in the United States, and more than ten million copies worldwide. These are unparalleled numbers for a book that still appears only in its original hardbound edition. The material in this book has been adapted into more than forty languages in more than two hundred different countries because it has reached a common chord that not only transcends international borders, but travels across cultural divides as well. Thanks to Hallmark Books, with the edition of *Mars and Venus In Touch*, this valuable message will now reach millions more.

I relay this to you not to boast, but to share with you my gratitude for the international acceptance of my very simple message: that men and women do have unique and fundamental emotional differences. Now, in this new millennium, if humankind can continue to honor that fact rather than ignore it, we will create a better world for the couples of today, and their children who in turn will be the couples and the parents of tomorrow.

I think the phenomenal success of *Men Are from Mars, Women Are from Venus* is due to the fact that it provided the right message, at the right time. Never before in our common human experience has the nature and the balance of the male-female dynamic been so deeply affected by sociological change as those changes that are sweeping the globe today. These changing roles, both in the home and out in the workplace, have caused considerable upheaval in society over the past quarter century. Because of these changes, the importance of understanding the differences that can divide men and women will never be greater than now.

In many of my subsequent books, I explore the different approaches men and women bring to love, in varying stages of life: *Mars and Venus in the Bedroom, Mars and Venus on a Date,* and *Mars and Venus Starting Over* each examine the values and desires that men and women bring to a relationship at a particular point of their emotional growth. The books then suggest problem-solving techniques for the issues faced at these times. In spite of all of the differences couples encounter, they should never forget that they have one common factor that keeps bringing them back together: They both share in a mutually exclusive love.

The world is filled with millions of loving, monogamous relationships in which both partners are frustrated because they feel they are not being heard—or understood—by their partners. I take great pride in the thanks bestowed on me by thousands of couples who claim that some of the simple communication techniques I have placed in my books have changed their relationships forever and for the better.

This said, we cannot allow ourselves to forget, that not every relationship is meant to last. Too often, I get letters to my advice column from both men and women who are determined to keep their one-sided relationships going, despite the obvious fact that they are getting no passion, love, or support from their partners. My advice has never wavered in its insistence that they realize the truth about their situation, and move beyond it with an open heart. Doing so will allow them the time and opportunity needed in recognizing a true soul mate.

Some of my advice is gender-specific. For example, he needs

to find a solution, and she needs to share; he needs acceptance and trust, while she needs caring and understanding. The simple truth is that we always had, and will continue to have, different needs. If we can learn to accept and honor that, the journey to lifelong love will be smoother and more rewarding.

Both you and your partner may be seeking a truly loving partnership. Desire, however, is half the job. The necessary communication tools are also needed.

The skills you both learned by reading this book will take time to integrate fully into your daily lives, and must be applied repeatedly in order to modify your behavior. Take the time every few weeks to reread sections of the book and reflect on how the concerns addressed here relate to the issues you are facing in your everyday life and relationship.

Past generations have faced great changes, and therefore great challenges. My hope is that future generations will honor the work that we did in setting new standards in the dawn of a new millennium of men, women, and relationships.